Contents

Youth Pastor

The Theology and Practice of Youth Ministry

Monday: Teacher
Tuesday: Friend
Wednesday: Recruiter
Thursday: Visionary
Friday: Administrator
Saturday: Teammate
Sunday: All of the Above

Houston Heflin

Foreword by Amy Jacober

To Karen,
Whose faithful love is an
experience of God's grace.

YOUTH PASTOR
THE THEOLOGY AND PRACTICE OF YOUTH MINISTRY

This book is printed on acid-free paper.

Library of Congress Cataloging-in-Publication Data

ISBN 978-0-687-65054-5

09 10 11 12 13 14 15 16 17 18—10 9 8 7 6 5 4 3 2 1

MANUFACTURED IN THE UNITED STATES OF AMERICA

Foreword

One of my favorite assignments in an introductory course on youth ministry is to ask the students to articulate just what a youth pastor is and what she or he does. The answers most often appear in list form, a random (and often rambling) sampling of elements students include so as to not leave anything out. The assignment is further complicated by my asking the question of identity. The struggle to respond shows itself in long philosophical discussions of identity wrapped in considerations of who one is or what one does. Which comes first? And the chicken-and-egg conversation takes over as the identity and the role of the youth pastor are considered.

Houston Heflin offers a way out of this conundrum. His work has led him to identify ten roles, which are grouped into five dyads that help us consider these roles specifically: (1) Approaches to Education—Evangelistic Missionary and Discipling Teacher, (2) Allocation of Time—Pastoral Shepherd and Organized Administrator, (3) Position of Advocacy—Bold Prophet and Compassionate Priest, (4) Focus on Relationships—Spiritual Friend and Equipping Recruiter; and finally, (5) Division of Responsibility—Visionary Leader and Faithful Teammate. Covering these roles helps youth pastors consider not only major areas within youth ministry but also the favoritism each holds. Translation: For right or wrong, we all tend to minister in ways that are most comfortable to us. There is nothing wrong with this as long as it is not *all* you do. Houston pushes us all to celebrate what we do well and naturally while addressing the areas we may neglect. Exploring these areas may take the form of looking at your own identity in ministry while seeking to strike a balance, or it may mean surrounding yourself with people who excel naturally in ministry areas where you are lacking.

Real-life stories and experience have been major factors influencing the reflection engaged in here. Each section and chapter begins with an indication of the heart and life of Houston. He is a seasoned youth worker who has given much thought to a balanced ministry and even more thought to the identity of those seeking this balance. He gives candid snapshots, including moments of great success and satisfaction and moments that have turned into learning opportunities over the years. His commitment shows in the number of years he has served. His insight is evident in the glimpses into his life that he offers. It will not be difficult for you as a youth worker to read his stories, close your eyes, and identify a similar scenario occurring in your own ministry now, one that has occurred in the past, or one that you may anticipate for the future.

While there are many ways to embrace a book, *Youth Pastor* lends itself particularly to three. First, this is not a book intended to offer "how to " instructions. Rather it is rich with opportunities for those who read it to slow down, pull out their Bibles, make notes, and discuss their findings with others. Houston wisely gives questions at the end of each chapter that help the reader to identify the major intent and focus of the chapter as well as how to practically apply in a variety of contexts what one has learned from the chapter. Second, the dyads in each unit encourage even veteran workers to look afresh on their ministry, giving them an honest opportunity to consider where life has settled and routine has taken over. For those new to ministry, these dyads provide a structure for making sure that major roles in ministry are not overlooked or neglected. Finally, Houston excels in offering scripture to accompany each and every element offered in this book. He never claims to be exhaustive but provides more than enough biblical support for each and every section. Scripture dominates his thought, paving the way for discussion and even full-blown Bible studies around every aspect of being a youth pastor.

Readers also can embrace this book in a variety of settings. First, for a youth worker, *Youth Pastor* can be a personal devotion (just check out all those scriptures!), a catalyst for organizing his or her youth ministry, or a Bible study guide. Imagine reading this with another volunteer or volunteer team. Using each section, consider the dyad and the roles within each. Where does your team excel and where does it have room to grow? Prayerfully consider the balance suggested. Even more, read this with a Bible nearby, asking the Holy Spirit to lead your team to see the principles in this book that will fit your situation as you seek guidance and strive for communal obedience.

Second, this book may find a comfortable home in classrooms. Because questions are already offered at the end of each chapter, it is ideal for use in leading group discussions. What questions would you add? What questions would your students add? Beyond the built-in discussion points, this book encourages all of us to consider, both philosophically and scripturally, the call to youth ministry.

Youth Pastor serves as a reminder that no one person is truly able to do ministry alone. God designed us to be in community, and while we may strive to be all things to all people, we will fall short. This is no reason for despair. In fact, it is reason to celebrate that in God's infinite wisdom a task was created that demands a team comprising diverse tendencies and strengths. Indeed, it is in a team that the body of Christ may best be seen and experienced.

One of my greatest lessons in ministry has come while serving a small church in Los Angeles. I am blessed with an amazing team, each of whom brings different strengths to the table. While we overlap in many areas, no single one of us could do the job on our own. My assistant youth pastor is clearly evangelistic and pastoral and excels as a spiritual friend. He is brilliant at spending time with teens and being certain that they are present and included even when they have seemingly disappeared. Another teammate is naturally organized and longs to equip students in a variety of ways. Her time with students is most often spent with the intent of passing on a skill or purpose. I could go on to describe the roles each of us fills based around Houston's dyads. Each of us brings different gifts, recognizing that we fall short in other areas but celebrating the differences we offer. Thus we feel no guilt, no stress to individually accomplish all the tasks of youth ministry. It truly is the best of all worlds.

Youth Pastor is an affirmation, philosophically and scripturally, that we are intended to serve as a team—that we may be released from the tyranny of competition and proving our worth over and above others whose tendencies differ from our own. It comes full circle, from beginning to end, with a call to consider who the youth pastor is and what the youth pastor does.

Amy E. Jacober
Associate Professor of Practical Theology and Youth Ministry
George W. Truett Theological Seminary

CHAPTER ONE
Becoming All Things in Ministry

The audacious hope of youth ministry is that imperfect disciples of Jesus can somehow inspire youth and their families to live like Christ. Taking care of our own spiritual maturity is difficult enough. Many of us amble toward Christlikeness with summit victories and dale defeats, but those who work with youth are given the responsibility—and blessing—of bringing others along. On this journey we are called to care for the souls of those traveling with us. This makes attending to our personal relationships with God even more important.

The appropriate genesis of any youth ministry is not a program for the spiritual formation of adolescents but a commitment to our spiritual formation as Christian adults and disciples of Jesus. Refusing to settle for a lukewarm likeness of Christ, those involved in youth ministry have an opportunity to become a primary instrument by which the Holy Spirit brings youth into a relationship with God. When we recognize the significant influence Christian adults play in the formation of adolescents, we set the stage for a more effective youth ministry that emanates from the spiritual maturity of its leaders (King 2006, 11).

Loving youth through adolescence is like flying in a plane that loses cabin pressure. The turbulence of the teenage years exposes a young person's soul to real threats. As ministers to youth, we need to be grounded in our relationship with God so we know how to respond to this turbulence. We must first place the oxygen mask of the Spirit over our own nose and mouth and breathe normally before we can adequately assist anyone else (Easum 2004, 28). If we have not first attended to our own spiritual health, we may discover we are of little use to those around us.

Know Thyself

Since our faith is based on belief in Jesus as God's Son, ministry in his name requires us to consider our identities as his disciples and ministers. The literature produced by youth ministry educators is replete with admonitions for youth workers to know themselves. Kenda Creasy Dean and Ron Foster (1998) suggest the work of youth ministry must be accompanied by "theological identity questions," including the introspective query, "Who am I?" (p. 32). Borgman (1997) offers similar counsel by suggesting that effective youth workers should consistently study and interpret not only the Bible and the culture, but also themselves. Such personal reflection will lead to knowing how to "be" as well as how to "do" (p. 58). Mike Higgs echoes this theme by proposing that identity precedes action in ministry. He notes that there is a temptation in youth ministry to have "an imbalanced emphasis on the outside of youth ministry—how we do it—and a corresponding neglect of the inside, or being—who we are as youth workers" (Higgs 2003, 15). Having a clear sense of identity gives us a new perspective on ministry goals and the responsibility of a youth pastor (Dunn 2000).

Ministerial Identity

Many people have appealed to well-known professions to describe the job of a minister. While these comparisons are somewhat helpful, they do not capture the heart of the calling. Terms such as "clinician (therapeutic metaphor), chaplain (institutional metaphor), coach (sports metaphor), entrepreneur, marketer, and strategist (business metaphors)" miss the mark of what it truly means to be a minister (Roxburgh 1997, 44). On one level it would be correct to say that a youth pastor is a program director, activities coordinator, chaperone, chauffeur, and janitor. Youth pastors certainly fulfill responsibilities in these areas at various times, but such roles also miss the mark. More accurate descriptors that reflect biblical roles and address the objectives of youth ministry could be used. Speaking to youth ministry educators, Jack and McRay (2005) said, "Our language is terribly important because it will convey to our students the callings and roles we value for ministry with youth. When they view their calling as an outworking of who they are deep within their souls, ministry becomes less of a job title and more of an outpouring of what God is doing in their hearts" (p. 70).

Defining the youth minister's identity is challenging because of the eclectic nature of the profession. Youth pastors serve among junior high and high school students, parents, volunteers, fellow ministers, staff, and elders. They work in church buildings, schools, homes, and camps, on athletic fields and mission fields. They are present amid celebrations, tragedy, victories, and mourning. They are on the front lines of spiritual battles for young people's souls. Ministry in these conditions requires a stomach for change and a desire to learn. It is no surprise, then, that youth pastors are a difficult bunch to pin down. They do not all look the same, nor can their identity be defined by any one role that they play (Neder 2001). Being a youth pastor requires skillfully juggling diverse roles in dissimilar contexts with people of multiple generations while enlisting others to join the effort. Paul recognized back in the first century this need for ministers to wear many different hats .

Becoming All Things in Youth Ministry

In his first letter to the Corinthians, Paul clarified that he was willing to remove any barrier that might stand between any group and the gospel. This required some dexterity. Paul testified:

> Though I am free and belong to no man, I make myself a slave to everyone, to win as many as possible. To the Jews I became like a Jew, to win the Jews. To those under the law I became like one under the law (though I myself am not under the law), so as to win those under the law. To those not having the law I became like one not having the law (though I am not free from God's law but am under Christ's law), so as to win those not having the law. To the weak I became weak, to win the weak. I have become all things to all men so that by all possible means I might save some. (1 Corinthians 9:19-22)

Paul understood the need for relevance in specific contexts. While among the Jews he lived like a Jew. Among the Gentiles he was a Gentile. To the weak (persons of low social status) he became weak and to the strong he was strong. Paul's goals were always "to win as many as possible" (1 Corinthians 9:19) and to serve in such a way that "by all possible means [he] might save some" (9:22). Paul had to play many roles and alter his approach for each unique situation he encountered. Ministry today is no different.

As there is no one-size-fits-all ministry program, there is no one role that a youth minister must play. This ministry requires contextualization and adaptability. It demands that youth workers change and grow and lead in new environments and amid unpredictable conditions. This high calling must be accompanied by constant prayer and reflection.

Profile of Ministry Roles

Based on the precedents set by God's servants in the Bible and the tasks beneficial to current-day youth ministry, I propose ten roles of professional and volunteer youth workers. These roles are: evangelistic missionary, discipling teacher, pastoral shepherd, organized administrator, bold prophet, compassionate priest, spiritual friend, equipping recruiter, visionary leader, and faithful teammate. I have grouped them into five identity dyads, each of which reflects a specific inclination of ministers.

The first pair of roles is educational. The youth pastor ministers to two groups of youth: those who are outside the church and those already on the inside. Youth workers might have tendencies as evangelistic missionaries who offer Christ to non-Christian teens or as discipling teachers who foster the spiritual growth of Christian youth. Time allocation frames the second pair. Pastoral shepherds are more likely to be found in schools, malls, and homes where teens are present, while organized administrators spend most of their time in an office or other location conducive to managing programs. The third set involves advocacy. Bold prophets represent God before the people and passionately declare God's truth, while compassionate priests intercede for the people before God. The fourth dyad focuses on relationships. Ministers may act as spiritual friends who spend a majority of time counseling and mentoring youth or they may serve as equipping recruiters who invest in relationships with parents and volunteers. The final pair involves the division of ministry responsibilities. Some youth

---

Approach to Education

Evangelistic   **Discipling**
Missionary   **Teacher**

Allocation of Time

Pastoral   **Organized**
Shepherd   **Administrator**

Position of Advocacy

Bold   **Compassionate**
Prophet   **Priest**

Focus on Relationships

Spiritual   **Equipping**
Friend   **Recruiter**

Division of Responsibilities

Visionary   **Faithful**
Leader   **Teammate**

---

pastors are able to function as visionary leaders. Others are faithful teammates who work better as part of a staff.

Justification for Roles

It is important to understand why multiple roles, and these ten in particular, are the paragon of ministerial identity. First, these roles have their origin in Scripture. They reflect the work of God's servants who have embodied these identities. Jesus himself fulfilled each of these roles in a unique way. He was an evangelistic missionary, sent by God to preach about the Kingdom (Luke 4:43). He was called "teacher" by his disciples and used the term to describe himself (John 13:13-14). He called himself a shepherd (John 10:11), feeling protective concern as an overseer of the sheep (Mark 6:34). He was an administrator who maintained focus on objectives (Matthew 16:21), solved problems (Mark 6:37-38), and directed disciples (Mark 6:39). People recognized him as a bold prophet (John 4:19; Matthew 21:11)—one who spoke the words of God (John 8:28), held people accountable for their sins (John 2:16), protested social injustice (Luke 4:18-19), and prepared people for things to come (John 2:19). He was a compassionate priest who knew the weaknesses of the people (Hebrews 4:14-16), interceded for them before God (Hebrews 7:25), and helped them receive forgiveness (Mark 2:5). He was a spiritual friend to the disciples (John 15:15) and demonstrated the greatest form of love by dying for them (John 15:13). He was an equipping recruiter who enlisted workers (Matthew 4:19) as he taught them (Matthew 17:19-21) and empowered them with resources for their work (Luke 24:49). He was a visionary leader inviting people to follow him (Mark 2:14) as he inspired them (John 6:67-68) and maintained focus on his goal (John 13:1). He was also a faithful teammate who did nothing without the blessing of the Father (John 5:19, 30).

The second reason for this list of ministry identities is that all ten of these roles are vital for accomplishing the objectives of youth ministry. Youth ministry is a Spirit-led discipleship process by which God works through Christian adults to lead teens into relationship with God and to Christlike maturity as part of the body of Christ, the church.

Third, living out these roles gives youth examples of ways that they can be in ministry. Young professionals who have been in one job for a few years will often lament the fact that they did not know all the professions they could have chosen to pursue. After they have invested thousands of dollars and years of education working toward one profession, they realize that another, more attractive job exists. It would be regrettable for someone to grow up without knowing about the many ways in which God uses God's servants. If youth only see youth pastors who are teachers or teammates, they may never be aware of how to use their gifts to become a visionary leader or an evangelistic missionary. By taking on all ten identities, youth pastors become models for teens of what they can become in God's kingdom (Boran 1996).

Finally, it is nothing less than an imitation of God for God's servants to play several roles. God is our Righteous Judge and Defender, our Merciful Father and Kinsman Redeemer, our Warrior and our Refuge. God's Son is Prophet and Priest, King and Servant,

Good Shepherd and Lamb. God's Holy Spirit is Counselor and Convictor, Teacher and Interpreter.

However, it is hardly feasible for any one person to become all things to all people *all the time*. Contextualization is key. When youth workers consider their identity in a specific context, they may get a clearer picture of their mission and a renewed enthusiasm for their work. Then they will bask in the blessings of the gospel (1 Corinthians 9:23) and, by God's power, accomplish the audacious hope of youth ministry.

Reflection

1. Whom have you known who has excelled at becoming "all things" for the sake of the gospel?

2. How have you seen youth ministers effectively live into each of these ten roles?

3. What are the defining experiences of your life that have helped you understand who you are?

Notes

Boran, G. 1996. *The role of the adult youth minister in youth ministry.* Ph.D. dissertation. New York: Fordham University.

Borgman, Dean. 1997. *When kumbaya is not enough: A practical theology for youth ministry.* Peabody, MA: Hendrickson.

Dean, K. C. and R. Foster. 1998. *The Godbearing life: The art of soul tending for youth ministry.* Nashville: Upper Room Books.

Dunn, R. 2000. Response to Lamports, "At bay in the fields of the Lord: A conversation about the disposition of youth ministry professors in Christian liberal arts colleges and seminaries" *American Baptist Quarterly.* 19 (1); 89-92.

Easum, William M. 2004. Put on your own oxygen mask first: Rediscovering ministry. Nashville: Abingdon Press.

Higgs, M. 2003. *Youth ministry from the inside out: How who you are shapes what you do.* Downers Grove, IL: InterVarsity Press.

Jack, A. S. and B. W. McRay. 2005. Tassel flipping: A portrait of the well-educated youth ministry graduate. *Journal of Youth Ministry.* 4 (1): 53-74.

King, Mike. 2006. *Presence-centered youth ministry: Guiding students into spiritual formation.* Downers Grove, IL: InterVarsity Press.

Neder, C. N. 2001. "Acting wisely: Programs, routines, and disciplines." In K. C. Dean, C. Clark, and D. Rahn (Eds.), *Starting right: Thinking theologically about youth ministry.* Grand Rapids, MI: Zondervan/Youth Specialties. 341-48.

Roxburgh, A. J. 1997. *The missionary congregation, leadership, and liminality.* Harrisburg, PA: Trinity Press International.

UNIT 1

Approach to Education

Evangelistic Missionaries and Discipling Teachers

Over the last three centuries ministry to youth has embraced two different approaches to teaching the next generation about Christ. One strategy is aimed at youth who do not know Christ and the gospel while the other focuses on youth already in the church. Both methods have been important to the history of youth ministry.

The beginning of modern youth ministry can be traced to the evangelistic work of Robert Raikes, who in 1780 began Sunday schools (Reed and Prevost 1993, 257). His ministry was an attempt to reach the impoverished street children of Gloucester, England, who were forced into labor throughout the week and were unable to attend school. While the initial focus of Sunday school was on learning language and math—skills the children missed out on during the week—as public education developed, the emphasis quickly shifted to biblical literacy and Christian teaching. This out-reach ministry spread, and churches around the world imitated it as a means of evangelism.

By the late 1800s youth ministry through the Sunday school had evolved so that some groups were turning their focus inward. Horace Bushnell's book, *Christian Nurture,* suggested that all children should grow up Christian and not know themselves to be anything else (Bushnell 1861, 10). He called on churches and families to pursue the ideal of assisting good children to be even more faithful followers of Christ. Out of this emphasis came groups such as the Young People's Association of the Lafayette Avenue Presbyterian Church of Brooklyn (1867) and Christian Endeavor (1881). These organizations had a primary audience of Christian youth and approached youth ministry as a form of discipleship for those in the church (Senter 2004, 48).

By the mid-1900s the pendulum was swinging back toward evangelism. Pioneers such as Jim Rayburn, who started Young Life in 1941, were more mission-focused (Cannister 2003b, 179). They structured youth ministry based on the observation that many teens were not growing up in Christian homes and therefore could not be nurtured as if they had. Others agreed with this assessment and formed groups such as Youth for Christ (1944).

While evangelistic ministry organizations were forming in the second half of the twentieth century, the position of full-time youth minister in the local church became more widespread (Bergler 2002, 60). These workers joined the lineage of servants whose focus was sometimes on evangelism but at other times turned inward on the discipleship of Christian youth. Evidence suggests that the tension continues. Mark Cannister, in 2003, conducted a study of 120 North American youth ministry professors, revealing an interesting discrepancy in how they view their discipline (Cannister 2003a, 75). Almost half (48 percent) said youth ministry is primarily educational. The next largest group, more than a third (38 percent), said that youth ministry is primarily missional. A small minority (3 percent) said that it is both missional and educational. The fundamental difference between these two approaches is the difference between teaching to make disciples (conversion) and teaching to mature disciples (nurture). The former helps those who are lost find salvation (justification), while the latter helps those who have been justified become more like Christ (sanctification).

Reflection

1. Has the youth ministry in your church focused primarily on Christian youth or on those outside the church? How is this an intentional or unintentional decision?

2. Is the current emphasis in your church a reflection of the youth pastor's personal gifts, the values of the larger church, or both? Who in your church has a vested interest in Christian youth? In non-Christian youth?

3. What new initiatives could be implemented to restore balance between what is currently being done educationally for the benefit of youth already in the church and the goal of reaching other types of teens?

Notes

Bergler, Thomas. 2002. The place of history in youth ministry education. *Journal of Youth Ministry*. 1 (1): 57-72.

Bushnell, Horace. 1861. *Christian nurture*. Grand Rapids, MI: Baker Books.

Cannister, Mark W. 2001. "Youth ministry's historical context: The education and evangelism of young people." In *Starting right: Thinking theologically about youth ministry*. Dean, Kenda Creasy, Chap Clark, and Dave Rahn, eds. Grand Rapids, MI: Zondervan/Youth Specialties. 77-90.

Cannister, Mark W. 2003a. The state of the professoriate: An empirical study of youth ministry professors in North America. *Journal of Youth Ministry*. 1 (2): 65-78.

Cannister, Mark W. 2003b. Youth ministry pioneers of the 20th century, Part II. *Christian Education Journal*, Series 3, 1 (1): 176-88.

Reed, James E. and Ronnie Prevost. 1993. *A history of Christian education*. Nashville: Broadman & Holman.

Senter, Mark H. III. 2004. Horace Bushnell, Theodore Cuyler, and Francis Clark: A study of how youth ministry began. *Journal of Youth Ministry* 2 (2): 31-52.

CHAPTER TWO

Evangelistic Missionary

After graduating from seminary, Rob Browne and his wife left their home in Atlanta, Georgia, and moved to Novosibirsk, Siberia, to share the gospel and plant churches. Despite their commitment and hard work, they were not accomplishing their goal of establishing growing churches with Christian adults. Willing to try something different, Rob volunteered one summer to help with another ministry in town called World Wide Youth Camps, which was short on workers. The response from the children and youth during camp was exactly what Rob had hoped for from the adults he served. The youth seemed more receptive to the story of Jesus and more willing to commit to lives of discipleship. So Rob made a decision. Instead of pouring more energy into adults, he would focus on the world's largest demographic available to be reached for Christ. He became the full-time Director of Russian Operations for World Wide Youth Camps. More than ten years have passed, and he is still in this position today, as a missionary—one who focuses on youth.

In the same way, youth pastors are evangelistic missionaries with a special emphasis on youth and their families. Although adolescence is a biological stage it is also a cultural phenomenon. From this perspective, "ministry to youth is a form of cross cultural evangelism. [Youth] have a unique system of processing theology, a unique set of developmental needs, and a peculiar code of behavior" (Jackson 2000, 40). The cultural peculiarities of youth do not stop there. Young people have a special language, territories for gathering, rituals, rites of passage, and iconic leaders who define the norms of the culture. Some have gone so far as to say that youth should be the primary missional focus of the church

(Borgman 1997, 29). At a minimum, the "principles that guide cross-cultural ministries around the world apply to youth ministry" (Clark 2001, 80). So what are some of those principles and what does an evangelistic missionary to youth look like?

What Is an Evangelistic Missionary?

A missionary is a representative sent across a boundary with something to communicate. An evangelistic missionary is a representative of God who carries God's words to the people of the world so that they can be reconciled to God (2 Corinthians 5:20)— in our case, Christian youth workers, compelled by the gospel, reaching not to a location on Google Earth, but to a ubiquitous tribe known as adolescents. To do this the youth pastor must address several theological identity issues (Dean and Foster 1998, 32). These include an understanding of God and Scripture, an understanding of those being reached, and finally, an understanding of ourselves as witnesses to the gospel (Borgman 1997, 37).

Know the Word of God

The first requirement for effective mission work is to understand Scripture. It is by the light of God's Word that we see God, know ourselves, and understand the world around us. More importantly, the Bible communicates the message of a God who pursues us with sacrificial love. As missionaries we carry that message to the world.

One day the Spirit led the apostle Philip to a traveling Ethiopian who needed someone to explain to him the prophetic words of Isaiah that he had been reading. Philip "began with that very passage of Scripture and told him the good news about Jesus" (Acts 8:35). Philip had a familiarity with the text the Ethiopian was reading, as well as an understanding of the good news of Christ. Whereas Philip was initially of seven men appointed to care for widows (Acts 6:3-5), he became known as "the evangelist" (Acts 21:8) because of his willingness to share the good news (Acts 8:5, 12).

When Paul met with the Jewish leaders in Rome, he faced a similar challenge. "From morning till evening he explained and declared to them the kingdom of God and tried to convince them about Jesus from the Law of Moses and from the Prophets" (Acts

28:23). Drawing from all parts of Scripture, he spoke about Jesus. Connecting verses and stories from throughout Scripture to the good news of Christ was a necessary skill for evangelists in the first century. Likewise, evangelistic missionaries to youth today will gain credibility as they encourage youth to search the Scriptures.

Know the Witness

In addition to knowing the Scriptures, missionaries should know themselves by taking an inventory of their own strengths and weaknesses. This should be a humble, honest assessment of gifts and abilities as well as insecurities, prejudices and sins. Understanding these things will equip us with knowledge of areas we can grow in, as well as tasks we could invite others to take responsibility for.

When Jesus sent out the seventy-two he said, "Go! I am sending you out like lambs among wolves. Do not take a purse or bag or sandals." (Luke 10:3-4). It may be that youth pastors carry bags and burdens of selfish ambition, fears, doubt, or self-righteousness (Hobgood 1998, 22). Like Achan's sin that resulted in Israel's defeat at Ai (Joshua 7:1-15), our own transgressions could obstruct others from experiencing victory in Jesus. As John the Baptist said, "He must become greater; I must become less" (John 3:30).

One of the most important things to understand about ourselves as evangelistic missionaries is that we are not alone. As many cross-cultural missionaries are part of a larger team, missionaries to youth are part of a team that includes adult volunteers, parents, and anyone else helping to share the gospel to youth in this culture. Youth workers are not saviors of the world. They are servants of God and partners with others who share in the mission. As Paul said, some will plant, others will water, but only God makes things grow (1 Corinthians 3:5-9). We may encounter youth early in their faith journeys and never know in this life if they choose to become disciples.

About a year ago one of our students set up a meeting for me with one of her friends. This friend was a Kurdish Muslim about to leave for college who had never known a Christian leader whom he could ask the questions he had on his mind. Sitting in the local coffee shop, he asked how Christians could claim God had a family and why there are so many Christian denominations that argue with each other. He also searched for an answer to the atrocities committed by the church over thousands of years. At one point he asked me, "Why do you believe Jesus is God's Son?" I was not exceptionally knowledgeable about Islam or the Qur'an, but I did want to have a conversation. I listened to him share about his beliefs, and I took the opportunity to tell him why I believed what I do. I do not know where this young man is today, but I pray he has encountered other missionaries who have continued to plant seeds of God's Word in his life and watered what is already there.

Know the World

In addition to knowing Scripture and knowing ourselves, missionaries must know the culture and the people being reached. Evangelistic missionaries take joy in celebrating the positive aspects of youth culture and are cautious about condemning it, especially without understanding it first. They remember that the gospel transcends culture and meets adolescents' greatest needs by bringing them into relationship with God.

The often-referenced, but nonetheless powerful, example of Paul in Athens is as an excellent illustration of the value of being aware of the culture in which we work. Paul met with God-fearing people in the synagogue but also went out into the marketplace and talked to anyone who would listen. After looking carefully at the city's idols, he used what he had learned about the people's beliefs as a springboard for a conversation about the Lord of heaven and earth (Acts 17:23). He even quoted Greek poetry (Acts 17:28) to connect with his hearers and point them toward God.

The Chronological Necessity of Missionaries

While every role is important in service to the Kingdom, it is a chronological impossibility for there to be discipling teachers without evangelistic missionaries. To paraphrase Romans 10:14, how can someone grow in Christian maturity if she has not first believed? And how can someone believe without first having heard the message of good news? And how can one hear the message of good news unless an evangelistic missionary has shared this gospel with her? One must first connect with those in the culture before helping them grow in Christlike maturity.

Support from the Church

In too many churches, once missionaries are overseas they are forgotten and the adage is confirmed that those things out of sight become out of mind. This has happened to too many youth ministers as well. Our residential missionaries need support from the church to do their jobs. They need prayers. They need finances and resources. They need opportunities to share the joy they have for this work. They also need servants to join the mission team. In addition to all of these, churches can instill value in their youth pastors by commissioning them for their service, soliciting reports about the progress of their work, and providing opportunities for youth pastors to find rest and renewal.

Commissioning

Many faith traditions ordain youth pastors for their work and should be commended for their vision. But even churches that do not usually ordain youth ministers could commission them, much as churches commission missionaries. The purpose for this is to affirm that youth ministry is mission work. We see such commissioning in the Acts of the Apostles. While the church was assembled in Antioch, worshiping God and fasting, the Holy Spirit called out Barnabas and Saul (Acts 13:2). After they had fasted and prayed, the other members of the church placed their hands on the two missionaries and sent them off.

Reporting

One of the most important things missionaries can do for the church is report back to their supporters about the ways that God is using them. The church needs to hear "victory stories" from those who have been touched by the gospel. All Christians need to be aware of how God, through the missionaries they have commissioned, has used their offerings of prayer and resources for the work of the Kingdom.

When Paul and Barnabas returned to Antioch, where they had been commissioned as missionaries, "they gathered the church together and reported all that God had done through them and how he had opened the door of faith to the Gentiles" (Acts 14:26-27).

Later, the Antioch church sent Paul and Barnabas to Jerusalem to settle a dispute. They told the apostles and elders in Jerusalem and the Christians they met on the way about "how the Gentiles had been converted" and "everything God had done through them" (Acts 15:3-4). The final time Paul returned to Jerusalem he "reported in detail what God had done among the Gentiles through his ministry" (Acts 21:19).

Our church family recently organized a fascinating worship assembly. During our time together three of our commissioned missionaries were on the phone, communicating with the congregation through the sound system. These servants from Kenya, Uganda, and Burkina Faso led aspects of the service as we shared in Communion together. They also spoke to the congregation about their work. These missionaries' passion was contagious and inspired others to serve. I wonder which teens will remember that morning as a formative experience that opened their eyes to the possibilities of serving as a missionary, either overseas or at home.

Furlough

At the end of their first missionary journey, when Paul and Barnabas reported back to the Antioch church "all that God had done through them[,] . . . they stayed there a long time with the disciples" (Acts 14:27, 28). Part of their work as missionaries was to periodically stop and rest.

As every week needs a Sabbath, every missionary needs a furlough—some period of rest to acknowledge that the work, or part of the work, is completed. Each year I take a mini-sabbatical between Christmas and New Year's Day. I go to a hotel, unplug the TV and phone, and sit. I typically write in a journal, read stories in Scripture I have not visited in a while, and think about the past and the future. It is a healing time because I can look back on the events of the past months and know that they are over. There is a sense of accomplishment in taking the time to pause and look back on your work. This mini-sabbatical is also a time of preparation for what is to come—a time for new dreams and stillness before the business of life takes over again with the start of a new year.

Youth missionaries need furloughs. They need times when they do not have teaching responsibilities, when they can participate in adult Bible studies or just take time to rest. They also need seasonal breaks after busy times of the year, whether after a summer full of camps and mission trips or after a school year packed with programs.

We see this concept at work in Mark 6: "The apostles gathered around Jesus and reported to him all they had done and taught. Then, because so many people were coming and going that they did not even have a chance to eat, he said to them, 'Come with me by yourselves to a quiet place and get some rest' " (Mark 6:30-31). After a season of work, the disciples returned to Jesus to tell him what they had done. Their efforts apparently warranted rest, so Jesus invited them to withdraw to be alone with him. After this time of renewal with Jesus, he sent them out again (Mark 6:45). When we spend time alone with the Word of God, it sends us out to tell what we have experienced.

Furloughs are excellent times to revisit our calling, recharge our souls, and reengage if we have lost connection with Christ. Terry McGonigal highlights Mark 3:14-15 as a model for evangelism in youth ministry. In these verses Jesus chooses apostles to be with him, to send out to preach, and to have the authority to drive out demons. "Everyone involved in evangelistic youth ministry must take seriously this priority of personal spirituality—of 'being with Jesus' before engaging in ministry activity" (McGonigal 2001, 131). Youth pastors must be evangelized before evangelizing. And after spending time with us, youth should be better equipped and inspired to share their faith with others.

Exit Strategy: Producing Missionaries

One objective of mission work is to teach the people whom you are leading and serving to be self-supporting and to develop leaders among themselves who continue the work. In youth ministry, the youth pastor is attempting to instill in teens the passion and skills necessary to continue growing by becoming evangelistic missionaries in their own right.

A well-planned international mission experience will often have an exit strategy: some plan whereby missionaries mark the end of their work in a country. An appropriate exit strategy for youth ministry would look slightly different. Instead of the youth pastor leaving, the youth leave, and not just to begin another life phase. They leave to take responsibility for fulfilling the Great Commission and becoming evangelistic missionaries themselves. For some this happens even before they leave your youth ministry.

When Melody was fifteen, she participated in a summer mission experience that paired high school students from local churches with at-risk eight-to-ten-year-olds for a week of camp. For seven days the high school students and their "little buddies" did everything together. They swam, went hiking, had Bible studies, and ate together. The job of the high school student was to intentionally pour out God's love on the child he or she was paired with, and the children typically ate it up. At the end of the week, when everyone went home there was always a great deal of crying because the teenagers and their buddies had bonded so deeply. As Melody sat crying and her new friend, Rosie, drove off, someone told her she would get over it soon; but Melody was determined that this week of camp would not be the end of her relationship.

Soon Melody got her driver's license and began picking up Rosie. They would go to a movie, go to church, or just hang out. It was not long until Rosie's sister wanted to come along. Then a couple of cousins and a neighbor began coming too. The group quickly outgrew Melody's little car, so she boldly went to the elders of her church and asked if she could use a church van to pick up the kids. They let her, as long as an adult would drive. A few kids became a few more kids, and then a large number of kids began coming to this church. Soon Melody had to start her own set of Bible classes at a little house near the church building to accommodate all the kids who wanted to be involved. Before long, three vans were needed. The children were mostly poor, mostly minorities, and completely unchurched. Although Melody had grown up in an all-white, middle-class church, it did not matter to the kids. They knew love when they saw it.

After graduating from high school, Melody decided to attend college in her hometown, mostly to stay with her now-blossoming ministry. While giving almost every moment of free time to the kids, she still managed to go to school, hold a job, and graduate in three years. Upon graduating, she had no idea what she was going to do. Then the church where she grew up hired her to help start a church for the families of the kids she loved. Today, Melody is married with four children, and her husband is the preacher at the little church she started. It still reaches out to those in poverty and those struggling with addiction, regardless of race or cultural background. Most of the people who attend the church have no idea it all began with a girl who, at fifteen years old, was an evangelistic missionary.

Compelled to Speak

There is wisdom in the dictum attributed to Saint Fancis of Assisi: "Preach the gospel at all times; when necessary, use words." The apostles of the early church, however, found words absolutely critical to their message. When Paul entered a city his usual custom was to enter the synagogue and proclaim the Word of God (Acts 13:5, 14ff.; 14:1; 17:1-2, 10-11, 17; 18:4, 19; 19:8). He refused to allow his actions to be the only communication, although his actions were vital to his message.

Paul's passion for Christ compelled him to speak. He was so convinced that his life of discipleship was worthy of imitation that he said to King Agrippa while on trial in Caesarea, "I pray God that not only you but all who are listening to me today may become what I am, except for these chains" (Acts 26:29). How serious are we about inviting others to discipleship? Do we really want them to experience what we have known? Is our passion that teens will know Christ and the power of his resurrection (Philippians 3:10)? If we are not serious about evangelism, we may need to spend more time with the story that led us to believe in the first place.

When Jesus commissioned the seventy-two disciples, he sent them in twos to every town he intended to visit. They were harbingers of his presence as workers gathering the harvest. Jesus instructed them, "Ask the Lord of the harvest, therefore, to send out workers into his harvest field" (Luke 10:2). The issue is not whether there are receptive hearts that will respond to the good news of the gospel. The crops will grow regardless of what we do. Rather, the issue is whether God's people will answer the call to be the workers who harvest these crops. May we have the vision of Christ to see that the fields are ripe for the harvest (John 4:35).

Reflection

1. Describe the cultural context of mission work in youth ministry, including the language, customs, and icons of youth culture. Who are the poets and philosophers for today's youth whom we must engage?

2. What challenges does your ministry face in reaching teens?

3. What types of youth are most receptive to your ministry? Whom could you be reaching that you are not currently?

4. If you wanted to evangelize the largest group of unreached youth in your area, what would need to change in your youth ministry and in your church?

5. If you were asked to report on the work of God among non-Christian youth in your area, what would you say?

6. What would be an appropriate way for a youth worker in your setting to go on furlough?

7. How has your church supported its "residential missionaries" (youth pastors)?

Notes

Borgman, D. 1997. *When kumbaya is not enough: A practical theology for youth ministry.* Peabody, MA: Hendrickson.

Dean, K. C. and R. Foster. 1998. *The Godbearing life: The art of soul tending for youth ministry.* Nashville: Upper Room Books.

Hobgood, William Chris. 1998. *The once and future pastor: The changing role of religious leaders.* Herndon, VA: The Alban Institute.

Jackson, Alan. 2000. Does the church need youth ministry? *American Baptist Quarterly.* 19 (1): 22-44.

McGonigal, Terry. 2001. Focusing youth ministry through evangelism. In *Starting right: Thinking theologically about youth ministry.* Dean, Kenda Creasy, Clark, Chap, and Rahn, Dave eds. Grand Rapids, MI: Zondervan/Youth Specialties, 125-40.

Senter, Mark H. III, Wesley Black, Chap Clark, and Malan Nel. 2001. *Four Views of Youth Ministry and the Church.* Grand Rapids, MI: Youth Specialties Academic.

CHAPTER THREE
Discipling Teacher

I will never forget the night during my sophomore year of high school when a new youth ministry volunteer began teaching at my church. Despite having parents who always brought our family to church early, on this particular Wednesday night, we were about twenty minutes late because of a school meeting. When my brother and I tried to enter the door to the youth room, we found that it was stuck, so I gave it a second push with my shoulder and it quickly opened as I stumbled into the room. The displeasure on our teacher's face was matched by his bitter words "Get out! And don't come back." Shocked and slightly embarrassed by his critical reaction, we sat in the parking lot until the youth meeting was over.

Our interruption of his lesson must have seemed to him like the work of unruly youth. He later apologized for misreading the situation and confessed to being more concerned at the time with demonstrating control of the classroom than offering hospitality. He added that what he was teaching by his actions was not what he intended to communicate. His transparency revealed his genuine interests, and I learned about his true motivation for serving in the youth ministry. He would later become a primary influence in my desire to enter ministry; but for a moment, this teacher had lost sight of his ultimate objectives and his actions followed suit. As discipling teachers, who teach young people in the church what it means to be disciples of Christ, youth pastors benefit from having a clear vision of what they hope to teach and who they desire their students to become. They will also benefit from knowledge of the biblical precedents of teaching through discipleship. But before we look at methods of discipleship in the Bible, we begin where good teaching starts. The first qualification for teaching is becoming a good student.

Learning: The Prerequisite to Teaching

The scene at Matthew's house must have been as disappointing to Jesus as it was shocking to the Pharisees. After inviting Matthew to discipleship, Jesus ate a meal at his house. While Jesus was getting to know Matthew's guests, the Pharisees asked the disciples, "Why does your teacher eat with tax collectors and 'sinners'?" (See Matthew 9:9-13.)

Jesus explained that the sick need a doctor more than the healthy do. Surely the Pharisees would agree that sinners and tax collectors were spiritually "sick." Then Jesus turned the tables by administering a prescription to the Pharisees, suggesting that they too were ill and quoting the prophet Hosea, "Go and learn what this means:" Jesus said, " 'I desire mercy, not sacrifice' " (Matthew 9:13). Their medicine was to return to the Scriptures and meditate on Hosea 6:6. Even though these Pharisees were religious teachers and experts, there was something they needed to learn.

Jesus was describing the divine expectation that learning precedes teaching and that teachers continue to be learners. Ezra lived up to such an expectation. He "devoted himself to the study and observance of the Law of the LORD, and to teaching its decrees and laws in Israel" (Ezra 7:10). He was a student-teacher, someone who studied and applied in his life what he learned before presuming to teach it.

Paul took this matter very seriously and asked, "You, then, who teach others, do you not teach yourself? You who preach against stealing, do you steal?" (Romans 2:21). Such inconsistency cannot continue in a teacher's life. A teacher must learn from the lessons she espouses.

The significant influence that teachers have on the formation of their students is one reason James cautioned that not many should presume to be teachers (James 3:1). He makes it clear that teaching in God's name invites stricter judgment. If the teaching we communicate or the example we portray detracts students from Christlikeness, then we have committed a heinous offense against God, who is passionate about his children's souls (Luke 17:2). Because "everyone who is fully trained will be like his teacher" (Luke 6:40), we must become disciples worthy of imitation.

Biblical Discipleship

Many people want to know how to teach. That is why books like *The Essential 55* (Clark 2003) make the *New York Times* Best Seller List and other books like *McKeachie's Teaching Tips* (McKeachie 2002) become best sellers among collegiate teachers. But what is the secret to teaching disciples of Jesus? Biblical teachers have left us some clues. Specifically, five student-teacher relationships shed light on what it means to teach a disciple. The relationships between Moses and Joshua, Elijah and Elisha, Jesus and Peter, Barnabas and Saul, and Paul and Timothy all illustrate teaching for discipleship. These examples come from the Law, the Prophets, the Gospels, and the early church. In all of these cases, the teachers (Moses, Elijah, Jesus, Barnabas, and Paul) carefully chose disciples who had received the Spirit of God. Second, the teachers trained their disciples for specific kinds of service. Third, the teachers nurtured their disciples with encouragement and love. Finally, the disciples set out on their own, imitating their teachers' behavior.

Character: Share the Spirit of God

The biblical teachers I have mentioned chose their disciples under the direction of God (Deuteronomy 31:14; 1 Kings 19:16; Matthew 4:18; Acts 11:25-26; 16:1-3). These pupils were receptive vessels for God's Spirit, which they possessed either before their call to discipleship or as they were commissioned for God's work. The presence in their lives signaled a transformation in character that happens during discipleship (Bennett 1995, 14), a transformation that for biblical disciples meant a life monopolized by the presence of God's Spirit (Galatians 5:22-23).

Except for Saul, who received the Spirit at the hands of Ananias, each of these disciples became recipients of God's Spirit through the blessing of their teachers. As we work among young disciples in ministry, part of our responsibility is to help them encounter God's gift-giving Spirit. But we cannot share what we do not first possess. Youth workers should demonstrate a life guided by the Spirit, with all its fruit (Galatians 5:22-23), the same Spirit that is known as "the Spirit of wisdom and revelation" (Ephesians 1:17).

Knowledge: Train for Specific Roles

The second trait common to discipleship relationships involves sharing specific information that prepares the students for future service. The biblical teachers named above offered opportunities for their disciples to acquire the knowledge the teachers possessed. These disciples were successful learners because they possessed a hunger for knowledge that made them teachable (Coppedge 1989, 54) and enabled them to develop specific competencies.

Joshua's training prepared him for military and spiritual leadership. Elisha's discipleship equipped him to become a prophet. Peter's education led him to preach and serve as a shepherd. Paul learned about mission work from his teacher, and Timothy studied to become a minister to churches.

In the mid-nineteenth century, an educator named Herbert Spencer took a critical look at what children learned and asked an elementary but brilliant question, "What knowledge is of most worth?" (Spencer 1896, 21). Spencer encouraged questions that challenged assumptions about educational content. From this perspective, we might ask, Which is more valuable to most teens, memorizing the periodic table of the elements or learning to balance a checkbook? In the same way, are we in the church really teaching those things that will serve our teens as they grow in discipleship? Which is more valuable to teens, memorizing the dimensions of the tabernacle or learning the story of the Good Samaritan? By no means should we neglect teaching the Bible to teens. After all, Luke in Acts commended the Bereans for studying the Scriptures (Acts 17:10-11); and Jesus said that the Sadducees were in error because they did not know the Scriptures (Mark 12:18-19, 24). All Scripture is useful for teaching (2 Timothy 3:16), but some sections of Scripture, such as the Gospels, occupy a position of prominence.

When I began in youth ministry, I created a curriculum plan with the intent of teaching every book of the Bible in detail to students as they grew up in our youth program. After a few years I realized my plan was somewhat misguided.

As I learned more about my students, it became apparent that I would need to extend my curricular plans to include the tough issues that teens face: the relationship between Christian living and participating in the surrounding culture; navigating relationships with friends, the opposite gender, parents, and siblings; under-standing world religions; and how to read the Bible. (If youth pas-tors simply tell youth what the Bible says without teaching them how to search the Scriptures themselves, they will do a great dis-service to the next generation of believers.) Often teaching requires us to begin with questions that come up in our day-to-day lives and then to look to Scripture for inspiration and understanding. Andy Stanley and Stuart Hall have suggested that students should fully understand seven principles when they graduate from a youth ministry: authentic faith, spiritual disciplines, moral bound-aries, healthy friendships, wise choices, ultimate authority, and putting others first (Stanley and Hall 2001, 10).

Relationships: Loving Disciples

A third characteristic of biblical discipleship is the loving com-mitment to, and encouragement of, disciples by their teachers (Donnelly 1998, 11). The biblical teachers I have named affirmed, loved, and encouraged their disciples.

Had they not been in relationships grounded in love, the disci-ples in these examples would have been nothing more than stu-dents. Instead, the teacher in each case was a model of support and encouragement for his disciples and formed a relationship with the disciple that reached beyond what is traditionally considered edu-cation. In so doing, these teachers empowered their disciples to venture out on their own as teachers and leaders.

A healthy relationship with an instructor fosters motivation (Deci and Ryan 2000, 71). This is particularly true of interactions between students and teachers outside the classroom setting (Jaasma and Koper 1999, 45). Jaasma and Koper discovered that the more out-of-class communication a student had with a teacher, the more likely it was that the student would be motivated in a tradi-tional educational setting with that instructor.

Interactive youth ministries where the teachers and leaders are involved in the lives of teens outside the classroom accomplish more than just building relationships. When adults and adoles-cents share life experiences such as mission trips, camps, retreats, and service projects, several important things happen. First, since the students have a connection with their adult leaders, when these adults teach, the teens are more likely to pay attention and participate. Perhaps more importantly, shared ministry experiences produce teachable moments in which adults can offer biblical wisdom to adolescents. Teacher-student relationships that include experiences outside the classroom reinforce the message that Christian principles apply to all parts of our life.

Skills: Lives Worthy of Imitation

The words of Jesus, the master teacher, reveal the goal of true discipleship. Preparing his followers to lead, Jesus washed their feet and directed, "I have set you an example that you should do as I have done for you" (John 13:15).

After being chosen, trained, and loved, the biblical disciples we have looked at set out to lead by imitating the examples of their teachers. After receiving confirmation that God was giving Israel the land of Canaan (Joshua 1:1-5), Joshua imitated Moses by sending out spies to explore the land before crossing the Jordan (Joshua 2:1). Joshua also turned away God's wrath from the people (Joshua. 7:25-26), as Moses had done before him (Exodus 32:11-14). Finally, as Moses prepared for his death by declaring the need for the people to choose between blessings and curses (Deuteronomy 30:19-20), Joshua prepared for his death by demanding the people make a choice between the Lord and the gods of their enemies (Joshua 24:14-15).

Elisha performed several impressive miracles that in many ways reflected the actions of his predecessor, Elijah. Elijah kept a widow's flour and oil from running out (1 Kings 17:14), while Elisha multiplied another widow's oil (2 Kings 4:1-7). Elijah predicted seven years of drought (1 Kings 17:1), while Elisha caused a valley to flood without water falling from the sky (2 Kings 3:16-20). Elisha revived a young boy much in the same way that Elijah had (1 Kings 17:21; 2 Kings 4:34). Finally, Elijah had struck the Jordan with his cloak so that he could cross the river on dry ground (2 Kings 2:8). Elisha later struck the waters with the cloak of his departed mentor and got the same result (2 Kings 2:14).

Peter walked on water (Matthew 14:29), healed the sick (Acts 9:34), preached (Acts 2:14-40), and raised the dead (Acts 9:40) as Jesus had done before him. Jesus' healing of Jairus's daughter (Luke 8) is strikingly similar to Peter's healing of Tabitha (Acts 9). Both Jesus and Peter responded to invitations to enter the home and both, upon entering, sent people out of the room (Luke 8:41, 51; Acts 9:38, 40). They each took the deceased by the hand and instructed her to get up (Luke 8:54; Acts 9:40-41).

Before Saul had become active in mission work, Barnabas was an envoy to the church in Antioch (Acts 11:22). The church in Antioch commissioned Barnabas and Saul for the special work to which the Holy Spirit had called them (Acts 13:2). Eventually, a disagreement caused Paul (Saul) and Barnabas to go their separate ways, each with his own disciple (Acts 15:36-41). What Barnabas first began by bringing a great number of people to the Lord as a leader of the mission to the Gentiles (Acts 11:24), Paul imitated, ultimately becoming the "apostle to the Gentiles" (Romans 11:13; Galatians 2:8).

Timothy's life was in many ways a reflection of Paul's. As Paul had been paired with Barnabas, Paul paired Timothy with Erastus and commissioned the pair to mission work in Macedonia (Acts 19:22). Paul commended Timothy as one who was doing "the work of the Lord, just as I am" (1 Corinthians 16:10). This young disciple later worked among the churches in close cooperation with elders as Paul had done in Ephesus (Acts 20:17-38).

As youth pastors we might ask, what practical Christian skills are we teaching? More specifically, what practical skills are youth learning from how we use our time and talents? How do we teach, pray, fast, study the Bible, and share the message of the gospel? Youth workers must provide a safe space in which youth can develop spiritual habits, learn how to live in relationship with other Christians, and learn how to make godly decisions about how to use their time, resources, and abilities. Such opportunities prepare youth for when they will venture out on their own.

Scripture gives several examples of effective teaching and learning for discipleship. The Bible tells of teachers who chose, trained, loved, and taught their disciples and of disciples who learned to imitate their teachers. These teacher-student relationships were defined by the presence of the Holy Spirit and give us a model of discipleship that is still valid today.

Moving to Maturity

The goal of discipleship is to lead others to maturity, guiding them from milk to solid food (Hebrews 5:12-14). Adolescents would benefit from adult Christians who communicate expectations for their development: men and women who not only affirm their position as beloved children of the Father but also challenge them to excel in faithfulness and growth. One way to do this is to surround students with Christian men and women who have journeyed with Christ.

Relationships that foster spiritual maturity work both ways. Just as students benefit from their relationships with teachers, so teachers benefit from relationships with their students. One particular relationship has taught me the importance of investing in relationships with youth and has shown me how a student can become a "co-discipler." I first met Jordan when he was in tenth grade, and our relationship flourished from the start. We have enjoyed years of experiences together: mountain climbing in Colorado, constructing a church building in Mexico, praying for a mutual friend to come to faith, organizing campouts and retreats, and leading worship together. Jordan is one of those students that made youth ministry joyful and brought me hope when discouragement would set in. I do not know all that he received from our relationship, but I know that I have learned about faithfulness from him. Today Jordan is a young married professional. Every Tuesday morning you can find us at the House Café, but we are not alone. We co-lead a small group of guys who get together to share breakfast and stories from life. Jordan has joined me in doing for some high school and college students what I hope I was able to do for him. Our small group is traveling life together under the Lordship of Jesus. We pray together. We attend one another's ball games and band concerts. We hold one another accountable to the life Jesus calls us to live. We study the Bible and ask hard questions. As was true for the first Christians, the centerpiece of our discipleship group is a weekly meal. But our meal is not in a home or a church building. We have found teaching and learning can happen quite effectively anywhere we come together.

The Contexts of Biblical Discipleship

Teaching for discipleship cannot be confined within the walls of a classroom. Jesus offered training and instruction for his disciples in several environments. He taught his disciples in synagogues (Matthew 4:23; 9:35; 12:9-14; 13:54), on mountainsides (5:1-2; 15:29-39; 17:1-13; 24:3; 28:16-20), in a garden (26:36), in homes (9:10-13, 23-26, 28-31; 13:36; 26:6-13), in fields (12:1-8), outside tombs (28:8-10; John 11:17-27; 20:11-18), in cities (Matthew. 11:1; 17:24-27) beside roads (20:29-34; 21:18-22), on a lake (8:23-26; 13:1-9; 14:25-33), and at the Temple (21:12-17, 23-27; 24:1-2).

He not only taught in multiple locations, he also taught in conjunction with several significant events: a wedding (John 2:1-11), a funeral (Luke 7:11-17), the giving of an offering (21:1-4), a storm (8:22-25), a trial (22:66-71), the sabbath (14:1-6), traveling (24:13-27), Passover (22:7-38), sickness (17:11-19), and meals (5:29-32). It was appropriate for the teacher who sent his disciples to be witnesses in "Jerusalem, and in all Judea and Samaria, and to the ends of the earth" (Acts 1:8) to train them for every setting they would encounter.

Youth ministry requires us to do discipleship in locations such as church vans, restaurants, airplanes, stadiums, cemeteries, and prisons. It may be one of the teaching ministries of the church most reflective of Jesus' example. The multiple contexts and environments where learning can occur, such as camps, retreats, and mission trips, not only help youth encounter Christ they also help train students for the settings and situations they might encounter as they get older and become discipling teachers themselves.

Our discipling relationships with students will flow from Christ's discipling relationships with us. As we grow in our relationships with youth, we must continue to respond to Jesus' invitation to discipleship and learning: "Come to me, all you who are weary and burdened, and I will give you rest. Take my yoke upon you and learn from me, for I am gentle and humble in heart, and you will find rest for your souls. For my yoke is easy and my burden is light" (Matthew 11:28-30).

Reflection

1. What are the barriers to discipleship in the church?

2. How do you, as a teacher, grow by continuing to learn? How has this continued learning been a resource for your ministry?

3. If you had only one hour to communicate with churched youth, what would you say to them? What messages do you plan to communicate to them in the coming year?

4. How can you incorporate more experiential learning activities into your ministry? What are some new locations or contexts in which teaching could occur?

5. Create a plan for the intentional discipleship of the youth in your ministry.

Notes

Bennett, David. 1995. The leader as . . . disciple. *Transformation*. 12 (4): 13-15.

Clark, Ron. 2003. *The essential 55: An award-winning educator's rules for discovering the successful student in every child*. New York, NY: Hyperion.

Coppedge, Allan. 1989. *The biblical principles of discipleship*. Grand Rapids, MI: Francis Asbury Press.

Deci, Edward L. and Richard M. Ryan. 2000. Self-determination theory and the facilitation of intrinsic motivation, social development, and well-being. *The American Psychologist*. 55 (Jan.): 68-78.

Donnelly, Edward. 1998. *Peter: Eyewitness of his majesty*. Carlisle, PA: The Banner of Truth Trust.

Jaasma, Marjorie A. and Randall J. Koper. 1999. The relationship of student-faculty out-of-class communication to instructor immediacy and trust and to student motivation. *Communication Education*. 48 (Jan.): 41-48.

Levine, Nachman. 1999. Twice as much of your spirit: Pattern, parallel, and paronomasia in the miracles of Elijah and Elisha. *Journal for the Study of the Old Testament*. 85 (Sep.): 25-46.

Lockyer, Herbert. 1958. *All the men of the Bible*. Grand Rapids, MI: Zondervan.

Madden, Myron C. 1988. *Blessing: Giving the gift of power*. Nashville: Broadman Press.

McKeachie, Wilbert J. 2002. *McKeachie's teaching tips: Strategies, research, and theory for college and university teachers*. Boston: Houghton Mifflin.

Mitchell, Margaret M. 1992. New Testament envoys in the context of Greco-Roman diplomatic and epistolary conventions: The example of Timothy and Titus. *Journal of Biblical Literature*. 111 (4): 641-42.

Spencer, Herbert. 1896. *Education: Intellectual, moral, and physical*. New York: D. Appleton & Co..

Stanley, Andy and Stuart Hall. 2001. *The seven checkpoints: Seven principles every teenager should know*. West Monroe, LA: Howard Publishing.

UNIT 2

Allocation of Time

Pastoral Shepherds and Organized Administrators

In 1996, the Link Institute of Huntington College conducted a survey at a national assembly of youth pastors. In response to an open-ended research question about difficulties in youth ministry, youth ministers said that time devoted to administrative duties permitted too little time devoted to youth (Strommen, Jones, and Rahn 2001, 36). When given the statement, "I cannot spend as much time with youth as I want," almost two-thirds (64 percent) agreed, implying that there are constraints on a youth minister's time that preclude personal ministry (Strommen, Jones, and Rahn 2001, 51).

In one sense, administration represents a high-task orientation while shepherding reflects a high-people orientation (Stevens and Collins 1993, 64). One focuses on programs while the other attends to people. This is not to say that administrators devalue people or that shepherding has no use for administration. Quite the opposite is true. After all, the shepherd must be organized enough to know how many sheep are in the flock, notice when one is missing and implement a plan to recover the wandering sheep (Luke 15:1-7). This may require employing a hired hand to supervise the sheep that the shepherd leaves behind. But while shepherding and administration complement each other, balancing the two is a difficult task.

Although administrative principles and programs are supposed to give people more time for ministry, too often those who perform the administrative tasks and oversee the programs do not have time for pastoral responsibilities. One study revealed that Protestant pastors spend almost one quarter of their time on administrative functions (Kuhne and Donaldson 1995, 151). The only other activity to receive more time was preparation for preaching. While the duties of a preaching pastor may be quite different from those of a youth pastor, the threat of drowning in administrative minutia is similar. Another study exposed a reciprocal relationship between the amount of time ministers spend in administration and the time they commit to personal ministry (Perl 2002, 173).

Responsible ministers understand the importance of tending to administrative tasks in order to achieve goals, but they always value people as a priority. "However powerful our management 'tools' become, they cannot replace the power of the towel and basin," say Shawchuck and Heuser (1996, 16) referring to Jesus washing his disciples' feet (John 13:1-20). Administration must serve the pastoral function of ministry and not overpower it. For this reason one must be careful not to devote too much time to administration. The size of the youth ministry, one's personal ministry style, and the specific needs of the ministry all influence the amount of time one should spend on administration. Discerning the appropriate balance between administration and pastoral ministry, or shepherding, demands reflection on the youth pastor's ministerial context.

Reflection

1. How do the administrative aspects of youth ministry enable or impede shepherding a pastoral ministry? In what ways does shepherding require administration?

2. If the youth pastor had no physical office, how would her work be different? In what ways does an office both support and detract from various forms of ministry?

Notes

Kuhne, Gary W. and Joe F. Donaldson. 1995. Balancing ministry and management: An exploratory study of pastor work activities. *Review of Religious Research*. 37 (December): 147-63.

Perl, Paul. 2002. Gender and mainline protestant pastors' allocation of time to work tasks. *Journal for the Scientific Study of Religion*. 41 (1): 169-78.

Shawchuck, Norman and Roger Heuser. 1996. *Managing the congregation*. Nashville: Abingdon Press.

Stevens, Paul R. and Phil Collins. 1993. *The equipping pastor*. Washington, D.C.: The Alban Institute.

Strommen, Merton, Karen E. Jones, and Dave Rahn. 2001. *Youth ministry that transforms: A comprehensive analysis of the hopes, frustrations, and effectiveness of today's youth workers.* Grand Rapids, MI: Zondervan/Youth Specialties.

CHAPTER FOUR
Pastoral Shepherd

One Saturday morning my wife, Karen, and I woke up to the sound of a hand banging against the front door of our townhome. I stumbled downstairs in my pajamas to the sound of continuous knocking and yelling. When I opened the door, a man I did not know was standing before me screaming that the building was on fire. I stepped out of the doorway and looked up at the roof to see huge flames and smoke billowing upward. Immediately, I ran upstairs and told Karen to get our four-month-old daughter, Matalee, out of the nursery and to meet me in the street. I grabbed my shoes, wallet, and car keys, and ran out of the house.

I met Karen with Matalee in the street moments later and heard the sound of fire engines just around the corner. For the next six hours we watched almost everything we owned burn or become ruined by smoke and water. But we were not alone on what would be one of the most difficult days of our lives. News spread quickly among the church family about what had happened. It seemed like only minutes after the firefighters arrived that some of the parents of my youth and some long-time youth volunteers arrived. Next the elder and his wife, who were instrumental in hiring us, came. Then another staff member arrived. Throughout the day more and more teens and adults from the church came to be with us during our ordeal. They certainly could not fix the problem and only later in the day were they able to be physically helpful by moving damaged things out of the house into a storage facility. The most important thing the church family did that day was to offer the ministry of their presence.

One elder and his wife took Karen and Matalee to the store to go shopping as I stayed with the fire-ravaged house. In the coming days and weeks we would need to obtain a lot of clothes and supplies. People from the church gave us money and offered us homes to stay in and cars to drive. Despite losing our home, we had everything we could possibly want. As a minister, there are days you feel unappreciated, when you feel as though you give much more than you receive from a church. On this particular day I remember thinking, "This church just loved us into staying many more years because today we became family." We felt like part of the flock because the church was shepherding us.

The Nature of Shepherding

The sheep-and-shepherd allegory has received a fair amount of attention in recent Christian literature as evidenced by books such as *Raising Lambs Among Wolves* and *Shepherding a Child's Heart* that offer instructions for parents and books on pastoral leadership such as *Feeding and Leading, They Smell Like Sheep, Like a Shepherd Lead Us,* and *Good Shepherds.* One of the reasons this metaphor is so prevalent in spite of our distance from, or lack of knowledge about, herding sheep is because of the Bible's dependence on the illustration to communicate who we are in relationship to God and one another.

At first glance shepherding appears to be for those who enjoy basking in the sun surrounded by meadows and cool streams—as long as they do not mind the droning of sheep. In reality, shepherding is a sophisticated art that requires many skills. Unfortunately, some of these skills can be fabricated. You have heard it said that wolves will hide in sheep's clothing, but some wolves don shepherding attire as well. A brief examination of biblical shepherds gives us some idea of who the real ones are. True shepherds have a relationship with the One Good Shepherd, they demonstrate selfless love for sheep, and when they lead, a flock of sheep follows.

Love the Chief Shepherd

Peter learned that the first question on the qualifying exam for shepherding is so important that it may be asked three times: "Do you love [the Chief Shepherd]?" (John 21:15-19). An affirmative response to this question is the first characteristic of true shepherds. They have learned from Jesus how to do their jobs. If we hope to lead a flock of youth without God's guidance, we will find ourselves wandering in wastelands more often than sitting by streams. After each of Peter's three loving confessions, he heard the directive to care for the sheep. The two greatest commandments remind us that loving the Chief Shepherd cannot be separated from loving his sheep.

Love the Sheep

In addition to loving their Leader, true shepherds display a deep love for their sheep. The mother of a newborn baby does not need instructions on how to love her child. The father who sees his little girl hurting knows how to embrace her and make it all better. A good neighbor knows how to share his possessions and his time to help someone in need. And, according to Jesus, a good shepherd loves his sheep. It is just natural.

Jesus said, "The good shepherd lays down his life for the sheep. The hired hand is not the shepherd who owns the sheep. So when he sees the wolf coming he abandons the sheep and runs away. Then the wolf attacks the flock and scatters it. The man runs away because he is a hired hand and cares nothing for the sheep. . . . I know my sheep and my sheep know me—just as the Father knows me and I know the Father—and I lay down my life for the sheep" (John 10:11-15). It is not enough for a shepherd to know the sheep. A hired hand knows the sheep, but cares nothing for them and runs away at the first sign of danger. The real shepherds love their sheep and make sacrifices for them.

There may come a time when defending the sheep requires every resource the shepherd possesses. Most youth pastors are not required to give up their lives for students, but many youth pastors have given so much of their time and energy to adolescents because these youth pastors love their youth. When a shepherd loves his sheep, the sheep know it, and they are more willing to listen and hear what the shepherd says. This is the third characteristic of true shepherds: the sheep recognize the shepherd's voice.

A Voice the Sheep Recognize

A true shepherd is surrounded by sheep who recognize his voice and respond to the shepherd's calls (John 10:4). Jesus said, "My sheep listen to my voice; I know them, and they follow me" (John 10:27). Sheep are able to hear and respond to the shepherd's voice because they spend time with the shepherd. He speaks to them and calls them by name (John 10:2-3). When the shepherd loves the sheep and the sheep know the shepherd, the sheep reap the benefits of food and protection. According to Jesus, the mark of a shepherd has nothing to do with the number of sheep in the flock but whether those sheep recognize the shepherd's voice and follow.

An Honest Metaphor

Have you ever considered the full implications of the shepherd-sheep metaphor? Those hapless, helpless creatures are us! In the Psalms, David wrote, "Know that the LORD is God. It is he who made us, and we are his; we are his people, the sheep of his pasture" (Psalm 100:3). We act like the animal whose name has come to mean "thoughtless follower." The metaphor is hardly complimentary. Maybe God calls us sheep to emphasize the disparity between our unworthiness and his love, because sheep have several less-than-flattering characteristics. So do we, and so do the teens we serve.

Sheep Are Prone to Wander

It is difficult to gauge the intelligence of animals, but you do not go to the circus to see the sheep do tricks. They are not trained to do anything. It is hard enough to make them listen and obey their shepherd. Often they thoughtlessly roam away. God said of Israel, "My people have been lost sheep; . . . they wandered over mountain and hill and forgot their own resting place" (Jeremiah 50:6).

I remember visiting Karen's family in Germany shortly after we were married and watching a shepherd out in the country with his sheep. The shepherd was leading his sheep from a large pasture to another field where they could graze, but a road separated the two areas. The shepherd was in front and the sheep were in a "V" formation behind him. When the shepherd got to the road he stopped, which told the sheep that they should stop too. While they waited for the traffic to pass, the sheep began eating the grass beneath them. Slowly, the tight collection of sheep dispersed as they sought out food to eat. Looking down, not watching where they were going, they were distracted and fell out of formation. People have a tendency to do that too.

Remember Martha's grievance against her sister: "Martha was distracted by all the preparations that had to be made. She came to [Jesus] and asked, 'Lord, don't you care that my sister has left me to do the work by myself? Tell her to help me!' 'Martha, Martha,' the Lord answered, 'you are worried and upset about many things, but only one thing is needed. Mary has chosen what is better, and it will not be taken away from her' " (Luke 10:40-42). Like Martha, we continually choose the tasks of this world over sitting at Jesus' feet. We are a distracted people who focus our attention on a multiplicity of insignificant commitments that will not influence eternity in any way except to keep us from entering God's presence.

Have you ever noticed that every part of God's creation obeys its Creator except humans? The light appears when God speaks, the waves stop at the shore, the grass grows in the meadow, the hummingbirds frantically flap, the moon appears at dusk, and it is all just as the Creator wills . . . except humans. What began in the garden continues today. "We all, like sheep, have gone astray, each of us has turned to his own way" (Isaiah 53:6); and when we wander, we are even more vulnerable to the enemy.

Sheep Are Completely Defenseless

Not only are sheep prone to wander, they are defenseless when they do. Many animals have some innate line of defense that protects them from attack. Worms can hide underground from birds, birds can fly away from cats, and cats can hiss and claw at dogs. Sheep, on the other hand, have no sharp teeth, no claws, no aggressive roar, no hole to hide in, and no speed to carry them away from danger. They are easy prey for their predators. The lion, the wolf, and the bear threaten the sheep, who are completely powerless to defend themselves.

Sheep Need Protection

Before slaying Goliath, David reported to Saul, "[I have] been keeping [my] father's sheep. When a lion or a bear came and carried off a sheep from the flock, I went after it, struck it and rescued the sheep from its mouth. When it turned on me, I seized it by its hair, struck it, and killed it" (1 Samuel 17:34-35).

Similarly, our "enemy the devil prowls around like a roaring lion looking for someone to devour" (1 Peter 5:8). On our own we stand little chance against that kind of foe. While doing ministry in Capernaum, Jesus saw the crowds and "had compassion on them, because they were harassed and helpless, like sheep without a shepherd" (Matthew 9:36). His response was to teach them, feed them, and help increase their faith. This faith then served as a shield to defend against all the "flaming arrows of the evil one" (Ephesians 6:16). Our youth need to grow into their faith so that they can protect themselves, but this must happen as they live among the flock, under the leadership of shepherds.

Israel's Shepherding Problem

You can learn a lot from what others do wrong. That is one of the reasons case studies are so useful in youth ministry. They allow us to make decisions and draw conclusions in a safe learning environment. Here is a case study I have used with my teens:

> You return home from school to find that your house is burning down and see your little brother or sister running back into the house to get something. As your younger sibling opens the front door, you are still forty yards away, and there is no possibility that he or she will hear you amid all of the commotion. What will you do?

Students will give a variety of answers, but invariably everyone will do *something*: call 911, run after the sibling, yell for help, and so on. (Some students with a pesky little brother will jokingly say they would do nothing; but, when it comes down to it, they would all do *something*.) The problem that God had with the shepherds of Israel in Ezekiel 34 is that they did *nothing* to help their sheep that were lost or in danger. This shepherding problem in Israel is an excellent example of what *not* to do.

When a flock of sheep scatters, the sheep are in danger of becoming food for wild animals (Ezekiel 34:5). And often the sheep are not even aware that they are lost or in danger. The same is true for youth. Consider the fourteen-year-old girl who has a Web site that discloses personal information, making it available to anyone with an Internet connection. Some sheep just have no clue that, in the open country without a flock or shepherd, they are easy prey. It is important to note that God holds the shepherds, rather than the sheep, most responsible for situations in which the sheep are at risk. The only thing worse than a scattered flock, or even one lost sheep, is a shepherd who knows about it but does not do anything (Ezekiel 34:6)!

The most fundamental responsibility of a shepherd is to tend to the flock that is under his care (1 Peter 5:2), but Israel's shepherds could not look past their own needs to see the needs of others. They did not strengthen the weak, heal the sick, or bind up the injured. They did not bring back the strays or search for the lost (Ezekiel 34:4). Not only did the shepherds of Israel not care for the sheep, they were actually exploiting them (34:2-3). They ruled them harshly (34:4), even driving away those who were weak (34:21). How many youth ministries have treated the "sheep" in their care in a similar manner?

True shepherds of youth spend time with youth and are involved in leading, tending, healing, and feeding the flock.

God's Shepherding Precedent

God compensated for the deficiencies in Israel's leadership by taking on the role of shepherd. God searched for the lost, brought back the strays, bound up the injured, and strengthened the weak (Ezekiel 34:16), because without a shepherd a wandering sheep will likely remain lost.

I remember the first time I felt really lost. I was in a crowded marketplace in Esfahan, Iran, when I was about four years old. Old enough to feel independent but small enough to lose sight of my parents, I wandered away from both them and my siblings. Then there was that moment: a moment when the Persian carpets, fruit stands, and metal wares ceased to capture my attention. All I wanted was the sight of my mom or dad, but I could not find them. I started to panic, walking faster, hoping to see them each time I turned a corner; but they were nowhere to be found. Suddenly, I felt a hand on my shoulder and I turned around to see my father standing over me. He had been watching me the whole time and when he noticed I was lost, moving farther and farther away, he pursued me until he caught me. God is like that. Prior to the Exodus, God promised to free the Israelites from oppression and bring them out of Egypt, making a covenant with them and leading them to a fertile land (Exodus 6:6-8). These shepherding traits did not escape the attention of the psalmist who later noted, "[God] brought his people out like a flock; he led them like sheep through the desert" (Psalm 78:52). God also assigned many shepherding duties to Moses, whom God had called as a leader and servant. Toward the end of his life, Moses prayed that God would "appoint a man . . . so the LORD's people will not be like sheep without a shepherd" (Numbers 27:15-17). Joshua succeeded Moses and still others followed Joshua until God "chose David his servant and took him from the sheep pens; from tending the sheep he brought him to be the shepherd of his people" (Psalm 78:70-71). Israel saw both good and bad shepherds lead them while the prophets predicted that another great leader was coming. This leader would be a ruler and a shepherd for God's people (Micah 5:2; Matthew 2:6).

Jesus, the Chief Shepherd

Immediately after Jesus' story of the lost sheep and the lost coin in Luke 15, we read about the lost son. The parable teaches that shepherds must sometimes embrace sheep that have rejected them or spurned their care. There are teens who have resisted God in their lives and rejected offers of love from the church, convinced there is nothing to be gained from Christianity or an involvement in a faith community. Generally, these students are unhappy and lonely but cling to their conviction that removing themselves from church is a better option than staying involved. Often their hearts are so hard that they will only return when they have experienced the harsh reality of life without a shepherd. In Jesus' parable, the father embraces the son who has returned then hosts a reception in his honor. In the same way, God is our host: preparing tables, anointing heads, and filling cups to overflowing (Psalm 23). Similarly, Jesus acted as both shepherd and host when he fed the 5,000.

Jesus and his disciples needed food and rest, but their ministerial duties would not allow it. A mass of people had followed Jesus, eager to learn from him; and Jesus looked on them with compassion because "they were like sheep without a shepherd" (Mark 6:34). Jesus responded by feeding the crowd with teaching; but when his disciples demanded that Jesus feed the people's stomachs and not just their hearts, Jesus the shepherd became Jesus the host. In Psalm 23 fashion he had the people sit down in green pastures (Mark 6:39) and removed any want for food they might have. With the scant resources of a child's plate, he prepared a table before them and their baskets overflowed.

Though we work in a different setting than Jesus and his disciples, the skills of shepherding are nonetheless beneficial for our ministries. Two shepherding tactics are especially pertinent to youth ministry. First, you may have discovered that some sheep are more prone to wander than others. A good shepherd knows who these sheep are and will pursue them when they stray. Pastoral shepherds exist precisely because sheep tend to wander off and put themselves at risk of injury or attack.

Second, a good shepherd is familiar with the wild animals most likely to attack the flock. In biblical times, sheep were attacked by lions, wolves, and bears—three animals that hunt in very different ways. For youth ministers, our "sheep" face the many temptations of adolescence. As shepherds, we must discern these temptations and help youth defend against them. We must do so with caution because, as Paul warned the Galatians, even shepherds are prone to be tempted and led astray (Galatians 6:1).

Reflection

1. Who are the teens in your ministry who consistently wander, get lost, get injured, or need special attention? What will it take for you to rescue them, bind their wounds, and meet their other needs?

2. What "wild animals" consistently attack your flock?

3. How can you ensure that you are accounting for each teen? What structures currently in place can help you account for all the sheep?

Notes

Anderson, Lynn. 1997. *They smell like sheep: Spiritual leadership for the 21st century.* West Monroe, LA: Howard.

Bubeck, Mark I. 1997. *Raising lambs among wolves: How to protect your children from evil.* Chicago, IL: Moody Press.

Fleer, David and Charles Siburt, eds. 2006. *Like a shepherd lead us: Guidance for the gentle art of pastoring.* Abilene, TX: Leafwood Publishers.

Fleer, David and Charles Siburt, eds. 2007. *Good shepherds: More guidance for the gentle art of pastoring.* Abilene, TX: Leafwood Publishers.

Frazee, Randy. 2001. *The connecting church: Beyond small groups to authentic community.* Grand Rapids, MI: Zondervan.

Gangel, Kenneth O. 1989. *Feeding and leading: A practical handbook on administration in churches and Christian organizations.* Grand Rapids, MI: Baker.

London, H. B., and Neil B. Wiseman. 2000. *They call me pastor: How to love the ones you lead.* Ventura, CA: Regal.

Sanders, J. Oswald. 1994. *Spiritual leadership.* Chicago: Moody Press.

Tripp, Tedd. 2005. *Shepherding a child's heart.* Wapwallopen, PA: Shepherd Press.

Wagner, E. Glenn. 1999. *Escape from church, inc.: The return of the pastor-shepherd.* Grand Rapids, MI: Zondervan.

CHAPTER FIVE

Organized Administrator

If you serve in youth ministry for any length of time, you are likely to hear both accolades and criticism from parents. What you are not likely to hear is a parent say, "You gave us too much information," "We had too much time to prepare for this event," or "You were too organized." Parents of youth want the program run with acumen. They want to trust that information is correct, to know that events will happen as planned and that they will end on time. In short, adults want, and youth ministry needs, organized administrators to guide the ministry.

Youth pastors recognize this need as well. In a Link Institute study, youth ministers identified training in administration and management as an area in which they desired professional development (Strommen, Jones, and Rahn 2001, 305). When ministers elaborated on this desire they mentioned a desire to grow in areas such as time management, making use of technology, delegating responsibilities, and using workers effectively. The ministers who participated in this study understood that youth ministry cannot be separated from administration.

Administration in Ministry

Administration is the organized supervision of managerial tasks that are required to maintain a functioning system. The people in the system conduct these managerial tasks as they work toward a common purpose. This purpose may be a sales goal for a company, educating students at a university, or winning a championship on a sports team. In the church, administration is a partnership with the people of the church to accomplish the objectives of God's mission through ministry. As Paul said, "[we] are the body of Christ, and each one . . . is a part of it. And in the church God has appointed first of all apostles, second prophets, third teachers, then workers of miracles, also those having gifts of healing, those able to help others, those with gifts of administration, and those speaking in different kinds of tongues" (1 Corinthians 12:27-31). While administration does not rank as high as the primary roles of apostles, prophets, and teachers, it is nonetheless an important tool of spiritual leadership, one that is vital to the church and imperative for effective leadership in youth ministry.

R. Alec Mackenzie identified five aspects of administration: planning, organizing, staffing, directing, and evaluating. While planning and organizing involve concepts and ideas, staffing, directing, and evaluating involve the leadership of people so that goals are met. We see all five aspects of administration in the life and work of Moses and Joshua. These two Hebrew leaders will serve as illustrations as we explore each aspect of administration and establish precedents for youth ministers as organized administrators today.

Planning

In 1838, Robert Mills designed one of the United States' historic landmarks. His concept followed the form of an Egyptian obelisk and measured over 555 feet tall. The actual construction of this monument began in 1848 as granite and marble blocks were stacked on the national mall. Ten years later, when the structure had reached 152 feet, construction stopped—not because the monument was complete, but because the money had run out. Twenty-eight years passed before construction resumed, and the monument was finally completed in 1884. If you look at the Washington Monument today, you can see that it was built in two stages. Jesus said that anyone who wanted to build a tower should, before laying the foundation, "sit down and estimate the cost to see if he has enough money to complete it" (Luke 14:28). The Washington Monument serves as a real-life illustration of Jesus' teaching. What could have been accomplished in fourteen years took almost forty because of poor planning.

Planning involves collecting information, identifying objectives, envisioning possibilities, predicting costs, and establishing strategies. When Moses and God spoke at the burning bush, they discussed not only God's plan to rescue the Israelites from Egypt and lead them to the Promised Land (Exodus 3:7-10), but they also developed strategies and procedures for accomplishing that objective (Exodus 4; 7:1). One such strategy involved sending spies into the land of Canaan to collect information about Israel's enemies. One of those spies, Joshua, would later use the same tactic by sending spies into Jericho.

Jesus' life, ministry, death, and resurrection were the perfect execution of God's plan. On the night before Jesus' arrest, John says that Jesus "knew that the time had come for him to leave this world and go to the Father" (John 13:1). Jesus knew the plan and followed through with it. Our knowledge of God's plan is what sets us apart as Jesus' friends instead of his servants (John 15:15). A servant does not know his master's business, but a friend is kept informed; so Jesus revealed many things to his disciples. He told them that he would die for them (John 15:13), that he would rise again (Matthew 16:21), and that after going to the Father he would prepare a place for them in heaven (John 14:1-3).

Planning in Youth Ministry

Planning in youth ministry demands both time and discipline. It requires us to find time amid busyness and interruptions to do the work of our ministries. It takes discipline to envision the future based on past events and present realities. When done properly, planning makes a youth pastor's job much easier. But planning is more than a way to make ministries more manageable. It is a responsible use of time to prepare for service in God's name. "Not planning is poor stewardship of God's future" (Halvorson 2004, 30).

The effect of planning on a ministry's finances is an excellent example of how planning promotes stewardship. When a youth minister plans ahead, she is more likely to find lower fares and discount rates for her group. It is when ministers scramble to work out the finances at the last minute that money is often lost or wasted. Each spring, mission-trip organizers can testify that summer trips fill up quickly. Those most affordable weeks of service are reserved first. In other words, those who plan ahead are rewarded and save money. Those who wait until the last minute end up paying more.

Organizing

The organization stage of administration deals with the structural decisions concerning people, time, and resources in the organization.

When the burden of leadership became too great for Moses to bear alone, his father-in-law, Jethro, told him to distribute some of the responsibilities he had taken on. Jethro suggested that Moses appoint community judges that would make decisions on simple cases and bring difficult cases before Moses. Jethro named the requirements for the position, and Moses recruited capable people who feared God, who were trustworthy, and who hated dishonest gain (Exodus 18:21-26). By creating the role of judge, Moses gave himself more time and energy to serve as the people's representative before God. This was also the case for the apostles in the early church. Because they were having trouble meeting the needs of all the widows in their care, they created a position for persons who were "known to be full of the Spirit and wisdom" (Acts 6:3) and who would serve the widows and free up the apostles to focus on the ministry of the Word and prayer. The apostles found seven men to do the job.

Organization also involves setting priorities and determining how much time to allot for different tasks. When one does not set priorities or structure one's time, one is less effective. When we do not structure our time, we run the risk of being seduced by things that are unimportant or having our time taken over by the demands of dominant people (MacDonald 1985, 74). "Management is the art of doing the important things and not doing the others. It is the art of not getting splintered" (Drucker 1972, 6). By organizing time, ministers are most likely to invest in those things that are most significant.

Organization and prioritization were evident in Jesus' ministry. He created specific positions of leadership for the twelve men who would be his disciples (Matthew 10:2-4). He chose the people of Israel as the initial recipients of his gospel (John 4:22; Mark 7:27; Romans 1:16). As he trained his disciples he admonished them to set priorities as well (Matthew 10:11-14). If the people of a particular town did not accept them, the disciples were to move on, shaking the dust off their feet on the way out.

One day Jesus approached a man, inviting him to discipleship. In a misappropriation of time, the man replied that he first needed to bury his father. In response Jesus said, "Let the dead bury their own dead" (Luke 9:60). Furthermore, "No one who puts his hand to the plow and looks back is fit for service in the kingdom of God" (Luke 9:62). The harvest is so plentiful that urgent tasks await us, and how we use our time is of the utmost importance.

Organizing in Youth Ministry

Six months into my first youth ministry position, I led a group of adults and teens on a youth ministry ski day. Living in the suburbs of Denver, Colorado, made it convenient to travel one hour up Interstate 70 to the various resorts of Summit County and enjoy a day of skiing. On this particular day some parents were prepared to drive the youth into the mountains. As we assembled to pray for our trip, one of the parents asked me "Where are the maps?" Maps were the furthest thing from my mind. Every driver there had made the brief trek into the mountains several times, but something about driving it together as part of a church-sponsored activity told this parent that there should be organization, structure, information, and maps. Even when people know how to get where they are going, a map provides a sense of security. Organization in ministry provides similar security. It is like a road map that tells you how to get where you are going, even if you have to take a detour. For youth pastors, such a map is necessary both for events and for curriculum.

Many ministers find it helpful to organize their educational plan with a scope and sequence of lessons that they have created months or years in advance of the actual teaching event. With a scope and sequence in place, you can easily insert new articles, illustrations, notes, and reflections into an existing structure. This simplifies your teaching ministry. When you are organized, you have the luxury of either implementing the plan you already have or going with something else. If you are not organized, your only option will be the something else. While God often works through spontaneity, preparing activities through which five, fifty, or five hundred youth will experience God often requires much time and attention to detail.

A youth pastor must also organize finances, allocating money to the programs and persons who will help the ministry accomplish its objectives. Depending on the congregation, the youth budget could range from a few hundred to tens of thousands of dollars. Managing resources on that scale demands organization and attention to detail. One must record expenses, complete check requests, file deposit sheets, and submit reimbursements. These tasks are necessary for effective ministry even if they do not fit into traditional understandings of ministry.

Staffing

Staffing involves enlisting qualified people who can be trained to perform a function. Aaron was the first staff addition to Moses' mission. God permitted Aaron to assist Moses because of Moses' insecurities (Exodus 4:14-16). Throughout the desert wandering, Moses mentored his young aide, Joshua, to be his successor (Deuteronomy 34:9). Finally, at God's instruction, Moses recruited one leader from each tribe to do reconnaissance in the land and return with a report of its characteristics (Numbers 13:1-3). Each of these staffing positions required an existing level of proficiency that the people who filled the new positions improved upon.

Jesus also staffed the position of disciple with the unlikely candidates he found as he walked throughout Galilee (Matthew 10:2-4). In a similar fashion, Paul's missionary journeys led him to Lystra where he found a young man named Timothy, whom the believers there spoke highly of. Paul enlisted Timothy's help by making him an apprentice (Acts 16:1-3). In each case the ministry leader added personnel strength to his cause through staffing.

Staffing in Youth Ministry

The junior and senior students at one church were meeting for a Bible study when they decided that they were unhappy with the youth ministry program. Among their complaints were the lack of unity in the group, the poor level of participation by their friends, and most importantly, the insufficient number of activities for the group to enjoy together. While a discussion like this has the potential to become a descending spiral of criticism without any productive result, the students felt enough dissatisfaction with their own behavior to seek a solution. At the next youth meeting the youth minister invited anyone who was interested to join her for lunch and an activity-planning meeting. She divided the sixteen students who attended into teams of four and gave each team the responsibility of planning one semester of youth ministry activities. In response to the student's desire for change, the youth minister created a "monthly planning team" and staffed it with those youth who were most interested in helping. These planning teams have since become an important part of that ministry.

Staffing is something youth ministers continually deal with. They must know what jobs need to be done and who has the talents to accomplish them, whether teens or adults. In each case the youth minister must evaluate the needs of the ministry and the giftedness of potential workers.

Directing

Directing people entails coordinating multiple workers in the most efficient way possible, especially during times of transition. This may include resolving differences between feuding groups, motivating workers, or facilitating change. We see such direction in Moses' alignment of tribes to motivate them as they marched through the wilderness (Numbers 2), in his blessing the tribes to continue with God (Deuteronomy 33), in his public blessing of Joshua to facilitate the change in leadership (Deuteronomy 31:1-8), and in his intercession before God on the people's behalf (Exodus 32:11-14).

Directing was also key to the ministry of Jesus, who lived as a portent of transition. Jesus actively directed his disciples by sending them out in pairs to preach the good news (Mark 6:7). From the cross he directed the disciple whom he loved to take care of Mary as his own mother (John 19:26-27). After his resurrection, Jesus reinstated Peter, who had denied him three times, and directed him with the commission to "feed my sheep" (John 21:17). Finally, at his ascension, Jesus directed the disciples to stay in Jerusalem until the Holy Spirit arrived (Acts 1:4).

Directing in Youth Ministry

Once a youth ministry has been properly staffed and relationships have been developed, the youth pastor needs to direct the people who are staffing the ministry. The youth minister must sometimes assign jobs based on skills; at other times, the youth pastor will have to direct people into certain roles needed to accomplish stated objectives, even if these people are not specifically gifted in those areas. In both cases, the youth minister is responsible for guiding and directing.

Directing also involves motivating youth ministry workers. Let me suggest several effective ways to do this. First, youth pastors can establish clearly defined roles and objectives for volunteer positions so that workers know their responsibilities and when they have been accomplished. Second, youth ministry volunteers are more likely to be motivated when they are equipped with resources and trained in the skills they will need to accomplish their objectives. Third, adult volunteers need opportunities to spend time with one another away from teens. Serving with youth often pulls volunteers away from interaction with other adults. Youth ministers should provide opportunities for their adult volunteers to meet, share experiences, and build relationships, thereby motivating one another to continue serving.

Finally, directing means facilitating change. The very heart of youth ministry involves helping youth become mature disciples of Jesus by embracing the transformation that makes them into new creations (2 Corinthians 5:17). Transformation and change also occur within the youth ministry as a whole as waves of students enter and graduate each summer. Youth workers can serve as a stabilizing presence for both individuals and groups who are experiencing change at a faster pace than they may desire.

Evaluating

Evaluating one's ministry includes establishing a reporting system, measuring results, and taking corrective action based on that information. Ministries and ministers must be periodically evaluated so that church leaders are aware of how resources are used and what objectives are being achieved.

As Israel first approached Canaan, Moses commissioned leaders to spy out the land and present an evaluation based on specific criteria (Numbers 13:17-20). They were to assess the soil, towns, trees, and fruit of the land. When the spies returned, Moses requested a report that led to an open hearing about their discoveries (13:26-33). Moses also had to correct his siblings Miriam and Aaron when they revealed their jealousy of their brother (Numbers 12) and to facilitate the punishment of Korah, who had rebelled against Moses (16:1-33). In both cases, Moses evaluated the activities of those whom he led and took appropriate corrective action.

Evaluating was also important to Jesus' ministry. His disciples, upon returning from their mission work, reported to Jesus all they had done and taught (Mark 6:30). Similarly, Jesus reported about his work to God the Father. Testifying about the completion of his mission, Jesus said to God, "I have [completed] the work you gave me to do" (John 17:4). Jesus informed his disciples that they too would have to give an account for the words they had spoken (Matthew 12:36), as all people will be required to give an account of their lives to God (Romans 14:12; Hebrews 4:13).

Evaluating in Youth Ministry

Perhaps the most frequent use of evaluating in youth ministry occurs when someone counts the number of people participating in youth ministry programs. Attendance numbers and roll sheets evaluate who is present and who is not and indicate whether the ministry is growing in numbers. In response to these evaluations, youth pastors often take the corrective action of contacting absentees. As a good shepherd knows when one sheep out of one hundred is missing, the observant youth worker will notice when individuals are not present.

On the other hand, this sort of evaluation is not always pleasing to God. David, for example, chose to count the men who were reflective of his military strength instead of depending on God to deliver Israel's army from its enemies (2 Samuel 24:10). If we use large numbers to boast about our success, then we have failed to understand the gospel. Paul, in fact, boasted of the small number of people he had baptized so they would not boast about following him but rather would follow Jesus (1 Corinthians 1:14-15).

Finally, evaluating in youth ministry happens when ministers and ministries engage in reviews. Annual reviews are a prime opportunity to evaluate the objectives of the ministry against the product. The review team can assess what aspects of the ministry are effective and evaluate the role of the youth minister in that setting. But this type of review should not be limited to an annual evaluation. Personal reflection and review should continually occur. Every day is an opportunity to challenge assumptions about why things are working and what needs to improve. It is a chance to ask questions about our habits, ask questions of adult volunteers and teens about their perceptions of the ministry, and talk with peers in ministry. Is something happening in the ministry that repels teens? Are you equipping parents for their roles? Are you incorporating youth into the larger body of Christ? Are the youth being formed as disciples? Have youth matured in their relationships with God and their families? Are graduates faithful to God and the church one, five, and ten years after they leave your ministry? The answers to these questions will provide valuable information about the effectiveness of your work. As God evaluated the creation and pronounced it good, ministers must take an objective look at the work of their hands. Those ministries or programs that are ineffective should be revised or discarded.

Divine Administration in Ministry: Feeding the 5,000

One of the clearest examples of Jesus' administration in ministry is seen in his feeding of the 5,000 (Mark 6:32-44). He went through each of the five stages of administration that we have identified.

Planning: When presented with the dilemma of the large crowd without food, Jesus challenged his disciples to "give them something to eat" (Mark 6:37). John's account of this episode tells us Jesus gave his disciples this instruction to test them—to see what they could envision. Jesus already had a plan for what he was going to do (John 6:6).

Organizing: Jesus then gathered information about resources. He needed to know how much food was available. This pre-meal accounting prepared the disciples to be astounded by the abundance of leftovers. Knowing his priorities, Jesus blessed and gave thanks for the bread before he broke and served the loaves.

Staffing: Enlisting the twelve disciples as his staff, Jesus created the position of server to help feed the people. This position was an important component of Jesus' plan because of the servers' joint roles as distributors of food and students of the object lesson that would occur when they picked up the food.

Directing: The directing component of Jesus' administration began when he told the apostles to feed the people and then to gather resources. Then he directed his apostles to have the people sit down in groups on the grass, which was necessary to accomplish the goal of feeding the group. Jesus then directed the disciples to set the food before the people.

Evaluating: The numeric details in this story are staggering—8 months' wages, 5 loaves, 2 fish, groups of 50s and 100s, 12 baskets of bread and fish left over, and over 5,000 people. This evaluation testifies to the abundance that Jesus produces.

Administration is important to ministerial efficacy. But it is a means to an end. If maintaining the system of administration becomes the end being pursued, bureaucracy has been created (Gangel 1989, 87). Because administration has a tendency to monopolize time and tempt some to forsake pastoral shepherding, this instrument of ministry must be kept in check as subservient to the purpose it supports. As Will Willimon has warned, "our greatest administrative challenge is to keep the important things we do from crowding out the essential" (Willimon 1995, 47). The threat is that the attention required to perform managerial duties can distract us from the more significant matters of personal relationships. With intentionality and moderation, organized administration can give us control of the busy schedules that so often detract from ministry.

Reflection

1. How are planning, organizing, staffing, directing, and evaluating present in your ministry? Which ones of these stages are you drawn to? Which ones do you spend the most time with?

2. How could more intentional planning improve your ministry? Create a plan for the use of your time over the course of one week and then evaluate the effectiveness of that planning.

3. Based on the evaluative information you possess (such as attendance reports, budget figures, feedback from participants) what needs to change for your ministry to be more effective?

Notes

Drucker, Peter F. 1972. Peter Drucker on church management: The act of doing the important. *Christian Ministry.* 3 (5): 5-12.

Gangel, Kenneth O. 1989. *Feeding and leading.* Grand Rapids, MI: Baker.

Halvorson, Mary, 2004. Planning. *Clergy Journal.* 80 (7): 28-30.

MacDonald, Gordon. 1985. *Ordering your private world.* Nashville: Thomas Nelson.

Mackenzie, R. Alec. 1969. The management process in 3-D. *Harvard Business Review.* 47 (6): 80-81.

Rowell, J. Cy. 1981. The skills, knowledge and tasks of the professional church educator. *Lexington Theological Quarterly.* 16 (April): 68-75.

Strommen, Merton, Karen E. Jones, and Dave Rahn. 2001. *Youth ministry that transforms: A comprehensive analysis of the hopes, frustrations, and effectiveness of today's youth workers.* Grand Rapids, MI: Zondervan/Youth Specialties.

Willimon, William H. 1995. Administration or ministry. *Christian Ministry.* 26: 47.

UNIT 3

Position of Advocacy

Bold Prophets and Compassionate Priests

Youth pastors must serve as advocates who speak for voices that may otherwise go unheard. Sometimes the voices needing to be amplified belong to the students in youth ministry. Other times the voice belongs to God. Advocates for God are the bold prophets who declare God's truth with confidence, anticipating that the people who hear this message will respond repentantly. Compassionate priests are advocates for the people who submit the people's cares to their loving God. They also anticipate a response, but from God through answered prayer. Although both serve as advocates, the prophet and priest have very different roles.

The prophet speaks from divine instruction to influence the actions of the people. As God's representative, the prophet spends time with God in preparation to come before an audience, often calling the audience to repent. One of the first full-time church-based youth ministers in North America epitomized the role of bold prophet.

Lloyd Bryant served as minister to youth at the Calvary Baptist Church in Manhattan, New York. In the 1930s, he organized large youth rallies several nights a week that were broadcast on the radio (Cannister 2003, 68). This prophetic voice for God to the masses of youth in the northeast was followed by another voice in the Midwest when Youth for Christ rallies began in 1944. At their Chicago event they enlisted a young preacher named Billy Graham to speak. The campaigns, youth rallies, and radio programs of the early and mid-twentieth century were vehicles for sharing the gospel with listeners and helping those people form relationships that would sustain them. The prophetic leaders of these events stand in contrast to others in youth ministry who took a more priestly approach.

Those functioning as priests are servants of the people and represent the people before God. As ambassadors, they spend time with the people they serve, often listening, in preparation to go before God with prayers of intercession for the community. The priest receives information from the people and takes it before God, often as the people are gathered in worship.

Evelyn McClusky, the founder of Miracle Book Clubs, was such a person. She used storytelling and a conversational style rather than lecture in her teaching and offered low-pressure invitations to salvation (Cannister 2003, 71). Her clubs met in homes near high schools that served as settings where teens could first form relationships with adults and then learn about the gospel. The adults in these clubs performed the priestly acts of intercession, blessing the teens, and helping them come to God in worship. This foundation created an environment in which to share the message of Jesus.

Youth need godly ministers who serve both as priests and as prophets. They must hear God's Word boldly proclaimed in creative and relevant ways while also having advocates who can speak for them before God, the church, and their parents.

Reflection

1. Is your youth ministry focused more on prophecy or intercession?

2. How have prophecy and intercession influenced the character of the teens in your youth ministry?

3. What are some ways to implement prophecy and intercession in your ministry and church?

Notes

Cannister, Mark. 2003. Youth ministry pioneers of the 20th century, part I: Frederick & Arthur Wood, Lloyd Bryant, Percy Crawford, and Evelyn McClusky. *Christian Education Journal.* Series 3, (1): 66-72.

CHAPTER SIX

Bold Prophet

Several years ago I had reconstructive jaw surgery to correct a cross-bite. Before the procedure the surgeon explained that he would break my jaw and then re-attach it with screws. He said that when I woke up my face would be swollen, I would be really sore, and I would have to eat soft foods like applesauce and mashed potatoes for a few days before resuming a normal diet. The reality I woke up to after the surgery was very different from what I had expected. The first thing I noticed as I came out of a sedated haze was that my mouth was wired shut. I learned that my mouth would be clamped for nine weeks. The staples of my diet during that time were chocolate milk and fruit juice, and I had to consume all of my food through a straw. Aside from the constant hunger and shortness of breath that is inevitable when one's jaw is wired shut, the most memorable aspect of that experience was what it taught me about serving in ministry. As a youth minister who could not speak, I felt powerless. I realized how dependent I was on the spoken word and how valuable speech is to prophetic ministry.

Tasks of Prophetic Ministers

The biblical prophets were a motley group who spoke the truth and called people back to God. They were known by names such as "seer" (1 Samuel 9:9; 2 Kings 17:13; Isaiah 29:10; 30:10), "man of God" (1 Samuel 9:6; 1 Kings 17:18, 24; 2 Kings 5:8, 14), "servant" (Jeremiah 7:25; Ezekiel 38:17; Amos 3:7), "messenger" (2 Chronicles 36:16), and "watchman" (Ezekiel 3:17; 33:7; Hosea 9:8). God's prophets served in a variety of settings, spoke to a diverse range of audiences, and performed a number of tasks that are relevant to

71

youth ministry: they proclaimed God's Word, exposed sin, pro-tested social injustice, and prepared others for what would come.

Proclaim God's Word

First, the prophets proclaimed the words of God. They were the "heralds of the ideal" who received messages from God and shared those instructions with the people (Petuchowski 1990, 184). From Moses to Malachi, God's word poured from the mouths of the prophets. Then Jesus appeared as the paragon of prophetic liv-ing. He not only spoke the words of God but also demonstrated them as the incarnational Word (John 1:1-5, 14). Jesus repeated the "very words of God" (1 Peter 4:11). In the same way, God compels prophets today who are emboldened by the substance of the mes-sage they carry. Implicit in this prophetic role is the responsibility to proclaim the message that has been received and nothing else.

By a decree in the Law, severe consequences were imposed on the prophet who claimed to represent divine will but spoke a mes-sage that was not from God (Deuteronomy 18:20). This truth is sobering for prophetic ministers. Youth workers must know God's Word if they are to proclaim it. The alternative is to invite a rebuke similar to the one Jesus hurled at the Sadducees because they were religious leaders but did not "know the Scriptures or the power of God" (Mark 12:24). Youth ministers must know the Scriptures, and then offer themselves as living sacrifices to God before claiming to know and proclaim God's will (Romans 12:1-2).

Proclamation is the means by which we bring God's story to the youth of each generation, all of whom deserve to know the words and works of God. The psalmist pleaded for this opportunity when he prayed, "Do not forsake me, O God, till I declare your power to the next generation, your might to all who are to come" (Psalm 71:18).

Unfortunately, adolescents pick up many competing messages through the sounds, words, and images of our culture; and many young people feel ill-equipped to discern which messages are true. But youth must know the truth so that they can make informed decisions and identify falsehoods that vie for their allegiance.

High school students in particular are old enough to wrestle with the challenging truths found in the Bible. God's judgment through the flood, the violent wars of Israel, the questionable actions of several people in Jesus' genealogy, and the passion of the Song of Solomon are examples of content most high school students can handle. We do a disservice to those we teach if we refuse to address the entire truth of God's Word when they are old enough to learn from it. While there will always be a "null curriculum" in our churches—material that is not taught—we should give careful consideration to what is omitted. Omitting too much results in missed opportunities. And we might be surprised to find that passages of Scripture we often overlook actually intrigue our students. But regardless of whether the youth are interested, they must know the whole truth that sets them free (John 8:32).

Studies have shown that teachers who present the material of a lesson in an enthusiastic way get a better response from students (Patrick, Hisley, and Kempler 2000, 221; Easton 2002, 65). Patrick, Hisley, and Kempler discovered that, following an enthusiastically taught class, students were more energetic, curious, and excited about learning. They also were more likely to privately read material related to what they had learned in that class. This has important implications for the teacher whose primary text is the Bible. Each class is an opportunity to facilitate a passionate lesson that motivates teens to read more from God's Word.

Point Out Sin

The biblical prophets not only proclaimed messages from God, they also exposed the wickedness of the people. John the Baptist played this prophetic role and learned the possible consequences of pointing out sin. John boldly condemned King Herod's immoral relationship with his brother's wife, Herodias, by proclaiming, "It is not lawful for you to have her" (Matthew 14:3-4). Herod responded by putting John in prison. He wanted to kill John but refrained because the people considered John a prophet. Only later, because of a vow he made to Herodias's daughter, Herod had John beheaded (Mark 6:26-27). In short, John exposed the sin of someone in power, and it cost him his life.

Like John, Samuel also had the difficult task of confronting a king. On one occasion, Samuel was delayed in joining King Saul and his troops at Gilgal. Instead of waiting for the prophet to arrive, Saul impatiently offered the burnt and fellowship offerings that Samuel was responsible for. Samuel arrived as soon as Saul had finished the offering and rebuked him: (1 Samuel 13:13). Samuel then told Saul that, because of his disobedience, God had sought out a man after God's own heart to succeed Saul as king. But even this successor needed a prophet to point out his sin.

After sleeping with Bathsheba and arranging for her husband to die in battle, King David was far from the heart of God. So God sent the prophet Nathan to rebuke the king (2 Samuel 12:1-15). By telling a cunning story about a heartless thief, Nathan metaphorically recounted David's actions and exposed the king's sin. This led David to lament his sinfulness and repent of his rebellion (Psalm 51).

The people of Nineveh also benefited from a prophet's strong rebuke. After Jonah's terse threat—that God would destroy Nineveh in forty days—all of the people of the city turned from their evil ways and their violence (Jonah 3:4-5).

Jesus denounced such people in the cities of Korazin, Bethsaida, and Capernaum because they did not repent when he preached to them (Matthew 11:20-23). Jesus also condemned some of the religious leaders of Israel, calling them "hypocrites . . . blind guides . . . whitewashed tombs . . . snakes" (Matthew 23:13-33), who preached one thing and did another. Jesus even had stern words for the beneficiaries of his ministry. To the crippled man whom Jesus healed on the sabbath, Jesus warned, "Stop sinning" (John 5:14). To the woman caught in adultery whom Jesus spared from being stoned by an angry mob, he said, "leave your life of sin" (John 8:11). In each case Jesus communicated an expectation that the person would replace his or her sins with acts of holiness.

In a postmodern culture where tolerance and relativism reign, young people often feel tempted to view black and white issues in shades of gray. What once was called sin has become "an indiscretion." Rebellion against God is called "a lapse of judgment." Personal opinion and the dictates of one's conscience garner more respect than God's Word. In this context we may be too timid in the face of sin to name it as such, much less effectively eradicate it. When biblical literacy among our youth seems to be in decline and the God-given gift of humor is used to conceal immorality, the world needs men and women of faith with moral conviction matched by moral living to tell the truth, regardless of who's listening.

Protest Social Injustice

The prophets of Israel frequently condemned the ways that people treated one another and "demanded the standards of justice outlined in the law" for those affected by inequality, prejudice, and discrimination (Wootton 1998, 17). Elijah prophesied against King Ahab's murder and exploitation of a countryman (1 Kings 21:17-19). Amos prophesied against upper-class women who oppressed those in need (Amos 4:1) and against all who would "trample on the heads of the poor as upon the dust of the ground and deny justice to the oppressed" (Amos 2:6-7; 5:11; 8:4-7).

Jesus joined the list of prophets who spoke against social norms that did not meet God's expectations. He touched lepers (Luke 5:13), commended the deeds of Samaritans (Luke 10:36-37; 17:17-19), affirmed the faith of the poor (Luke 16:22), accepted children (Matthew 19:14), praised the faith of a Canaanite woman (Matthew 15:28), ate with tax collectors and sinners (Matthew 9:10), and healed on the Sabbath (Luke 6:9-10). The blind, the lame, the social outcast, and even the deceased were not excluded from his presence. Jesus introduced a radical social order that was not defined by economics, class structure, health, or age. Instead, it was established on "justice, mercy and faithfulness" (Matthew 23:23).

Youth ministry should be no different. It is unfortunate that those most needing the acceptance and love of a supportive Christian peer group are often rejected because they fail to meet that group's standards. While adolescent culture often makes judgments based on beauty, wealth, and status, the church must welcome all people. This begins with youth workers and churches modeling Christlike acceptance of all teens and culminates with the youth in that ministry accepting one another with the love of Christ.

Prepare Others for What Will Come

The fourth common task of the prophets was to prepare their audiences for the reality of the future (Mass 2001, 233). Samuel prepared Saul for the news that God had chosen another man to succeed him as king; Nathan prepared David for the news that Bathsheba's son would not live; Huldah told the royal court about Judah's impending destruction (2 Kings 22:14); Agabus prepared people for Paul's arrest (Acts 21:10-11); and John the Baptist told the Judean countryside that the Messiah was coming. Like Paul Revere, riding across Massachusetts to proclaim the advance of the British for war, John walked through the desert with a message that the Christ had come to bring peace (Luke 3:1-6; Matthew 3:1-6). "Prepare the way for the Lord" (Matthew 3:3), he said, and the people came out of the cities to repent in preparation.

Jesus carried on the legacy of the prophets by foretelling many things. He warned the disciples that he would go to Jerusalem, suffer, be killed, and then rise from the dead (Matthew 16:21). Jesus also told the disciples that in this world they would see trouble (John 16:33), and that the Jerusalem Temple would be destroyed (Matthew 24:2). Each of these has occurred, verifying Jesus' identity as a prophet. God supplied Israel with a test to assess prophetic authenticity. If what a prophet said did not come true, then Israel would know that the person was not speaking for God (Deuteronomy 18:21-22). In the same way, ministerial prophets would be wise to consider what future they are preparing their students for.

In one sense youth ministry is about preparing students for what will come. Specifically, youth ministry owns a share in the responsibility for equipping students for faithful service once they leave high school. Youth pastors can facilitate this preparation in several ways.

First, pastors prepare students for what will come by telling them the end of the story. It is no coincidence that God concludes the New Testament with the message of victory, offering hope to the martyrs and strength to the oppressed. As those in search of identity and direction, young people today need that kind of hope. They need to know that by claiming Jesus they join the winning team.

A second method of preparation is practicing spiritual disciplines. If adolescents develop spiritual habits now, they will be better prepared for faithful service when they leave high school. At an age when most people focus on the present, students need someone who will direct their eyes down the road toward a life with Christ when they are older—a life they can nurture while they are still young. We can accomplish this by training teens in habits that will not only serve them now but also mold them for the future.

Finally, youth ministers prepare students for future discipleship by encouraging them to participate now in the life of their congregation. Students who engage with the larger faith community in worship, prayer, fellowship, service, teaching, and evangelism will not be shocked to discover when they are older that these practices are expected of adult disciples of Jesus. The poor rates of church attendance after graduation may be an indictment of youth ministry's inability to incorporate students into the church at younger ages (Gibson 2004, 7). One way to prepare students for their future in the church is to teach them how to be the church today.

Jesus, the Great Prophet Foretold

When God gave the Law to Israel, God vowed to raise up a prophet from among the people to speak the very words of God (Deuteronomy 18:18). When John the Baptist preached in the wilderness, some of the priests and Levites asked him, "Are you the Prophet?" (John 1:21). Even the Pharisees considered it possible that John was the coming prophet (John 1:25), despite John's emphatic declaration that he was not (John 1:20). Between John's testimony and Jesus' miracles, it became clear that Jesus was the one whose coming had been foretold. After Jesus' miraculous feeding of the 5,000, the crowd declared, "Surely this is the Prophet who is to come into the world" (John 6:14). Others reached the same conclusion after Jesus spoke on the last day of the Feast of Tabernacles in Jerusalem (John 7:40). Those in Nain who witnessed Jesus raise a widow's son to life knew that a great prophet had appeared among them (Luke 7:16). The two disciples traveling to Emmaus on the day of the Resurrection told their companion that Jesus was "a prophet, powerful in word and deed before God and all the people" (Luke 24:19).

During Jesus' conversation with the Samaritan woman at the well, he revealed his knowledge of her sexual immorality. In response to what must have been a staggering moment, the woman replied, "I can see that you are a prophet" (John 4:19). The people who were in Jerusalem during Jesus' triumphant entry into the city shared this conviction. While the people of the city asked, "Who is this?" the crowds responded, "This is Jesus, the prophet from Nazareth in Galilee" (Matthew 21:11). It is no surprise then that Jesus performed actions like those of the prophets before him. He proclaimed God's word, pointed out sin, protested social injustice, and prepared others for what would come. On some occasions—such as when he cleared the Temple, spoke with the Samaritan woman at the well, and preached in Nazareth—Jesus modeled all of these aspects of prophetic ministry in one setting.

Clearing the Temple

In a bold act of prophetic indignation, Jesus cleared the Temple. Making a whip out of cords he drove out both animals and people, scattering coins and overturning tables (John 2:15). To ensure that his actions were not misunderstood, he proclaimed God's Word and reminded the people, "It is written," . . . " 'My house will be called a house of prayer' " (Matthew 21:13). He contrasted God's expectation with the current actions of the people. Pointing out their sin he said, "But you are making it a 'den of robbers' " (Matthew 21:13). This may have been in response to the injustice of selling overpriced animals and other items to be sacrificed in the Temple. When his authority was questioned, he prepared the people for a future event that would validate his identity: "Destroy this temple, and I will raise it again in three days" (John 2:19).

Samaritan Woman at the Well

On another occasion Jesus spoke with a Samaritan woman at a well near the town of Sychar. He proclaimed God's Word by saying, "If you knew the gift of God and who it is that asks you for a drink, you would have asked him and he would have given you living water" (John 4:10). The Samaritan woman knew neither the gift of God nor Jesus' identity, two things she would quickly learn. Jesus explained to her the gift of eternal life (4:13-14) and revealed to her his identity as the Messiah (4:26). During the discussion he pointed out her sin and said, "You have had five husbands, and the man you now have is not your husband" (4:18). A stranger who happened to be a Jewish male had laid bare an embarrassing secret of her seemingly private life. Yet he continued his conversation with her, a Samaritan woman. Despite her past, her current living arrangement, and animosity between Jews and Samaritans, Jesus ministered to her. Finally, he prepared her for what would come by testifying, "A time is coming . . . when the true worshipers will worship the Father in spirit and truth" (4:23). Jesus proclaimed

God's future by preparing this woman for worship that is defined not by location, but by the heart of the worshiper.

Preaching in Nazareth

A final example of Jesus modeling all aspects of prophetic ministry is his return to his hometown of Nazareth toward the beginning of his ministry. He stood in the synagogue on the sabbath and proclaimed God's Word from Isaiah (Luke 4:16-19). He then revealed to the people their sin of disbelief and told them they would demand a sign before they would believe (Luke 4:23). Later Jesus would say that a "wicked and adulterous generation asks for a miraculous sign" (Matthew 12:39). The content of his speech revealed his concern for justice, as the good news would be preached to the poor, prisoners and the oppressed. Finally, he prepared the people for what would come when he said, "Surely you will quote this proverb to me: 'Physician, heal yourself!' " (Luke 4:23). This prediction was fulfilled at Jesus' crucifixion as the rulers sneered saying, "He saved others; let him save himself" (Luke 23:35). The soldiers at the Cross followed with the taunt, "If you are the king of the Jews, save yourself" (Luke 23:37).

On each occasion, Jesus' speech and actions represented God's will and message to the world. And in each case the response of the listeners was different. Those at the Temple were likely confused and surprised, the Samaritan woman became a witness of Jesus the Messiah in her hometown, and those in Nazareth wanted to stone Jesus. These varied reactions to Jesus' prophetic ministry remind today's ministers that not everyone will be receptive to their service.

Prophets Are Rejected

Whether from misunderstanding, fear, annoyance, or disdain, many prophets are rejected by their listeners. Jesus found rejection early in his ministry when a synagogue full of people in Nazareth became furious and drove Jesus out of town with the intent of throwing him off a cliff (Luke 4:28-29). While Jesus successfully eluded his opponents' grasp in Nazareth, he willfully submitted to their clutches in Jerusalem. Following in the footsteps of Israel's former prophets, he endured persecution and offered his life for the ones who were rejecting him (Matthew 23:37). If history repeats itself, ministerial prophets, including youth workers, who speak confidently for truth will elicit harsh and calloused criticism. But as the biblical prophets relied on God's power to accomplish their mission, we have nothing less to help us with ours.

Reflection

1. How have bold prophets shaped your identity as a minister?

2. What prophetic messages do your students need to hear? What are some practical ways that you can prepare students for their future as disciples of Jesus?

3. What sins have gone unchecked or overlooked in your group that might compromise your mission?

4. What are the risks of speaking prophetically to teens? What are the risks of being prophetic with parents?

5. Create a plan for an intentional retreat to be alone with God and God's Word in stillness, quietness, and solitude.

Notes

Easton, L. B. 2002. Lessons from learners. *Educational Leadership*. September: 64-68.

Gibson, Timothy S. 2004. Congregational connectivity: The key to keeping youth in the church. *Journal of Youth Ministry*. 3 (1): 7-14.

Mass, Robin. 2001. Theological framework for youth ministry: Repentance. In *Starting right: Thinking theologically about youth ministry.* Dean, Clark, and Rahn, eds. 229-41.

Patrick, B. C., Hisley, J. and Kempler, T. 2000. What's everybody so excited about?: The effects of teacher enthusiasm on student intrinsic motivation and vitality. *The Journal of Experimental Education*. 68 (Spring): 217-36.

Petuchowski, Jakob J. 1990. Faith and works in the biblical confrontation of prophets and priests. *Judaism*. 39 (2): 184-92.

Wootton, Janet. 1998. *Prophets, priests and queens: An exploration of traditional terms used for the people of God with reference to their development throughout scripture and their appropriate use in worship and study today.* Lecture given at the Cheltenham and Gloucester Ecumenical Series for the end of the WCC Decade, the Church in Solidarity with Women, 19 February 1998.

CHAPTER SEVEN
Compassionate Priest

At ten o'clock on Thursday night the waiting room at Children's Medical Center was packed with people. So many had gathered that the hospital staff was getting uncomfortable. It was not common for anyone other than the family of patients to be around at this hour, so the hospital staff was not sure what to do. But those who had gathered knew exactly what we were doing.

The past four days had been a roller coaster ride for seven-year-old Tatum and her family. Their trauma began when the family rushed back to a Dallas hospital from a family vacation because Tatum was growing increasingly sick and eventually became completely unresponsive.

On Monday they were told that Tatum's liver was shutting down, that she was in a coma and that she might only have a few days to live. Tatum's family's only hope was to put her on the liver transplant list with the knowledge that a liver could come "any time, or not for months." And if a liver did arrive, it would need to meet certain health, size, and blood type qualifications.

At this point the church began to mobilize. One family with two little girls took Tatum's younger sister into their home. Another family organized meals to take to the family in the hospital. Still others called church members to pray. People from the church also met at the hospital. Everyone seemed moved to do something, including Tatum's immediate family, who began testing to see if anyone might meet the criteria to be a liver donor. (Unlike kidney transplants where the donor gives one kidney and keeps one kidney, a living liver donor gives half of his or her liver.) Tatum's uncle, however, met all of the requirements and immediately volunteered to undergo preparation for the intense and risk-laden operation.

As the surgery approached, Tatum began to decline. The doctors gave her 24 to 48 hours before they would lose her because her brain was swelling and they feared brain damage. They decided to put everything on hold until they could do a brain test. If there were only slight damage they would proceed with the transplant from the uncle. If there was major damage they felt it was unwise to risk the uncle's life and there would be no hope.

Thursday night everyone waited for the word about Tatum's brain test. Tatum's parents had gotten little sleep over the past 5 days, and understandably so. By ten o'clock that night the hospital waiting room was packed with over 75 people and enough food to feed twice as many. The hospital staff finally reached their limit and approached Tatum's father, David, to tell him only family members are allowed in the hospital at this hour, to which David replied, "These people *are* my family." The staff escorted the entourage onto another floor, where there was an empty classroom. As we left, one woman, who was sitting alone while waiting for a relative, curiously analyzed our group. Someone asked if she would like something to eat. Grateful for the gesture, this woman asked, "Who *are* you people?"

We were the church, assembled in a hospital, to cry with our friends, to bring them food, to sit with them, and to be present during their time of trial. We were gathered to pray for the life of this little girl we all loved and to ask that God's peace beyond understanding would be real for these parents who might suffer the worst pain that parents could experience. This was a church of priests. Tatum's father told God that night that whether or not Tatum lived, "We will keep our faith in you." That prayerful testimony sent some to their knees and served to reorient people's emotions from fear to faith in God.

In the middle of the night, a donor liver became available. A little child's life ended that night and the liver was sent to Children's Hospital for Tatum. Early Friday morning the doctors performed the liver transplant and three days later, on Sunday, Tatum emerged from her coma and began communicating. She is a healthy little ten-year-old today.

Priests help people navigate life's unexpected turns by offering stability and consistency. On that Thursday night in the hospital, the priesthood emerged in unexpected ways. The church served this role for Tatum's family, but her father became a priest for the church because he pointed people back to the only dependable source of strength to lean on: God.

The Creation of a Priesthood

God's creative activity that began in Genesis continued into Exodus with the creation of a new group of servants called priests. God introduced this role while entering into a covenant relationship with the people of Israel as they were gathered at Mount Sinai. Clarifying the parameters of the relationship, God said to Israel, "If you obey me fully and keep my covenant, then out of all nations you will be my treasured possession. Although the whole earth is mine, you will be for me a kingdom of priests and a holy nation" (Exodus 19:5-6). This began the sacred relationship that branched out to touch all people. God later specifically designated Aaron and his sons to be priests for that holy nation (Exodus 28:1).

The creation of this special role was a gracious gift (Numbers 18:7) because the people needed a representative in "matters related to God" (Hebrews 5:1). As an advocate for others, a priest's primary purpose is to facilitate the people's relationship with God through intercession, by helping the people bring offerings to God, by facilitating worship, and by blessing the people.

Intercession: Speaking for the People

Moses was a prophet of God and a judge for the people, but he also interceded as the people's priest. When Israel created the golden calf, Moses prayed to God, " 'Turn from your fierce anger; relent and do not bring disaster on your people.' . . . Then the LORD relented and did not bring on his people the disaster he had threatened" (Exodus 32:11-14, 30-32). Moses again interceded when the Israelites stood at the edge of the Promised Land but believed the bad report of the ten spies who wanted to return to Egypt. There he prayed, "In accordance with your great love, forgive the sin of these people, just as you have pardoned them from the time they left Egypt until now" (Numbers 14:19). Throughout the desert wanderings Moses prayed for the people after they grumbled against God (Numbers 21:7). In all these cases, God showed the people mercy; but intercession is not a guaranteed way to restore relationships. Abraham repeatedly interceded for Sodom; but after listening to Abraham's case, God still destroyed the city (Genesis 18:22-33). When Moses prayed for Israel after they had worshiped the golden calf, God did not destroy the entire nation, but the people were still punished.

As Jesus "always lives to intercede" for the saints (Hebrews 7:25), so we have a responsibility to intercede for those who are struggling with sin and rebellion against God. There is an intercessory component to praying for those who need forgiveness of sins. "If anyone sees his brother commit a sin that does not lead to death, he should pray and God will give him life" (1 John 5:16).

Compassionate priests look on the people with compassion. In the context of youth ministry, priests must recognize that teens will make mistakes that adults have been making for centuries. Not only that, teens will make the same mistake repeatedly even when they have a seemingly obvious way to avoid it. This priestly work demands that we have patience to suffer with teens and love them enough not to leave them alone in their pain or their sin.

As advocates, biblical priests stood between God and the people when God's law demanded the people be destroyed. Other times they stood between God and the people when the people lashed out at God, but their function as advocates did not stop there. They also interceded in conflicts among the people. When Miriam was struck with leprosy, Aaron interceded for her before Moses (Numbers 12:12); then Moses interceded for her before God (12:13).

In every case, priests intercede to encourage relationships. For youth ministers the intercession could involve a relationship between a teen and God, a teen and parent, a teen and the law, or even a teen and the church. A youth minister may be the only voice teens have among those who might otherwise never hear what God is doing through them.

Brad was in middle school and was the neighbor of a student in the youth ministry. He came to church for the benefit to his social life; after all, there were girls at church. When he abruptly stopped coming, the youth leaders discovered he was in a juvenile detention facility across town because of his alleged participation in a crime. These youth workers immediately contacted Brad, as well as his mom, and began praying for him.

For the court proceeding to determine his sentence, several adults had written letters to the judge informing her of the effort Brad had made to attend church, and they testified to the positive influence the church had had on his life. One of these adults was James, who had a special relationship with this student and wrote a compelling letter to the judge on his behalf. James did not expect the judge to remove the punishment, nor did he necessarily want her to. James just wanted her to know that someone believed in Brad and had hope that his life could change. When the verdict came, we learned that Brad would serve a six-week sentence in juvenile detention and we all knew it was much shorter than it could have been.

Over the next six weeks James frequently visited Brad in juvenile detention to read the Bible and discuss Brad's future. As they talked it was obvious that Brad's greatest need was not reconciliation with the friends he had disappointed, or even with the authorities. He had rebelled against God and needed a mediator. Brad knew what he had done was wrong and did not need to hear that from anyone. He needed someone to stand beside him as he endured the consequences of his actions. He needed someone who would not further condemn him. He needed a priest and found one in James, who had interceded for him before the judge and then helped him travel the path back to God.

Priests serve because something needs to be addressed in a relationship. At times sin divides relationships. Other times relationships break because of divorce or even death. The ministry of our presence and compassionate listening may be the most evident offering we make during these times, but they can be matched with prayerful intercession on behalf of the person's suffering. We need to communicate God's promise of peace beyond understanding, but we must resist the tendency to use trite words that harm more than heal. Sometimes silence is more precious than gold.

One night, as my wife and I were hosting another couple for dinner in our home, we got a call from a teen. She was almost incoherent from her sobbing, but we understood that she was driving to the hospital because her sister and dad had been in a car wreck. We left our children with our gracious guests and sped to the hospital. When we arrived, the doctors were informing the family that the sister, with a few broken bones, would be fine but that the father probably would not survive. What happened next has become etched in my mind. My wife wrapped her arms around this teen as she lashed out in agony to God and screamed, "Why? Why?" at the top of her lungs in the hospital waiting room. With empathetic compassion Karen just held on tight and cried with her.

The priests of Israel knew the weaknesses and the sufferings of the people. As humans aware of their own sin and suffering in life, they wrapped their arms around others with compassion in hope that these people would eventually find their way back to God.

Sacrifice: Accepting Offerings

The Israelite priests were also responsible for leading the people in making sacrificial offerings to God. God told them, "Tell the Israelites to bring me an offering. You are to receive the offering for me from each man whose heart prompts him to give" (Exodus 25:2). The people gave their sacrifices to the priests so that the priests could offer them to God. The apostles played the same role in the early church. "For from time to time those who owned lands or houses sold them, brought the money from the sales and put it at the apostles' feet, and it was distributed to anyone as he had need" (Acts 4:34b-35).

Youth ministers, as priests, can help teens understand two important concepts about sacrifice. First, we still need to bring offerings to God. The contribution, or collection, of financial resources is important not only to our relationship with God as a sacrifice but also to caring for others through ministry. This is something to be done thoughtfully. Although priests were told to bring the best offerings before the Lord, some offered sacrifices that were not holy (Malachi 1:6-14). God had little patience for these "useless fires" (1:10) and cursed anyone who had something holy to give but offered the leftovers instead (1:14).

A second important lesson for teens when it comes to sacrifice is that the offering God desires above all others is the gift of ourselves to God. We are to offer our bodies as "living sacrifices, holy and pleasing to God" (Romans 12:1). Instead of offering an animal as a sacrifice, our calling is to imitate Jesus, who offered himself. Paul taught these things to others, saying, "God gave me to be a minister of Christ Jesus to the Gentiles with the priestly duty of proclaiming the gospel of God, so that the Gentiles might become an offering acceptable to God, sanctified by the Holy Spirit" (Romans 15:16). In order for people to become the offering, they must be taught. In some cases modern priests have a responsibility left formerly to the prophets: proclaiming the gospel.

If we, as priests, are going to motivate God's people to make sacrifices, we must also be confessional and transparent. We can do this by admitting mistakes, sharing struggles, and communicating honestly about our journey with God. Priests offered sacrifices for themselves first and then for the people because they could not deny their own sinfulness. As priests today, we assist in the spiritual formation of others by admitting our own struggles and continuing on our journey with God. We are not without sin, so any attempt to help others gain reconciliation with God must begin with an honest look at the timber that obstructs our own vision (Matthew 7:3). I learned this lesson a few years ago.

It was the first year that our church staff conducted annual reviews. These reviews identified our individual strengths and weaknesses as perceived by our coworkers in ministry. I was somewhat surprised to find the following statement at the top of my list of areas in which I needed improvement: "Shares compassionate concern for those in grief and crisis." When I read it, my initial thought was to defend myself by recounting hospital visits and pastoral conversations with teens, as if those things inherently made me more compassionate. But my fellow staff members helped me identify an area of my ministry that had not fully matured. My heart wants to show compassion, but I don't always follow through with my words and actions. I am still working on this area of ministry, in part by consistently confessing my weakness and sinfulness in prayer.

Worship: Leading Praise

The third task of Israel's priests was facilitating worship. Whereas Old Testament priests were fitted with a breastpiece and other divine garb, the ornament of priests today is more likely to be a guitar. Like Kenaniah, the head Levite, who in David's reign led the people in singing because he was skillful at it (1 Chronicles 15:22), today's priests are frequently worship leaders. My friend Dan is one such priest. After college he served as a youth pastor for seven years while also leading worship. He later transitioned to focus on congregational life, worship, and pastoral (priestly) care for the church. If someone is sick, Dan knows about it. If someone is in the hospital, he has been there. If there is a request for prayer, Dan prays. He never shares gossip or speaks negatively about anyone. He's the person most likely to shed a tear in the assembly for someone who has experienced God. Although people may not think of him as such, Dan is a priest for his church family.

Romans 12 reminds us that we offer ourselves to God whenever we engage in "spiritual worship" (12:1). By leading worship, we enable others to offer themselves to God. Today's priests not only lead singing, they also administer the sacraments—namely baptism and Holy Communion—and facilitate all the disciplines that lead people to God, such as accountability, confession, and giving. The priest Zechariah, the father of John the Baptist, fulfilled his priestly duty by burning incense inside the temple while "all the assembled worshipers were praying outside" (Luke 1:10). Hilkiah, the high priest who rediscovered the Book of the Law during Josiah's reign, sought God's instruction on how to interpret the book and destroyed the objects devoted to false gods (2 Kings 22:1–23:25). These events began a reformation in Judah that pointed people back to God.

Neither Zechariah nor Hilkiah led singing, but they nonetheless enabled worship. Today's priests may be surprised to find that the simple act of helping teens understand their identities as Christians facilitates these teens' worship.

Blessings: Bless the People

The final responsibility of the priests of Israel was to bless the people. When Aaron and his sons began their ministry as priests, they first made sacrifices to atone for their sins and the sins of the people. Then Aaron blessed the people (Leviticus 9:22) as he and Moses entered the Tent of Meeting. When they emerged from the tent, they once again blessed the people (9:23). But even before God gave formal instructions to Israel's priests, the precedent of priestly blessings had been set.

The first priest mentioned in the Bible is Melchizedek, king of Salem. He brought out bread and wine to share with Abraham after the patriarch defeated his enemies. Before accepting Abraham's offering, and before praising God, Melchizedek blessed Abraham, saying, "Blessed be Abram by God Most High, Creator of heaven and earth" (Genesis 14:19). Later God gave Aaron and the priests specific instructions for blessing the people. They were to speak these words: "The LORD bless you and keep you; the LORD make his face shine upon you and be gracious to you; the LORD turn his face toward you and give you peace" (Numbers 6:24-26).

Our blessings today may look and sound different, but they contain many of the same elements of Israel's blessings. Trent and Smalley have suggested that blessings contain five ingredients: meaningful touch, a spoken message, attaching high value to the one being blessed, picturing a special future for the one being blessed, and making an active commitment to help fulfill the blessing (Trent and Smalley 2004, 30). Blessings are appropriate for all occasions. We can offer blessings before mission trips, on birthdays, before major events such as the first day of school, or before youth leave home after graduating. There are also other, more frequent opportunities to bless youth, such as the end of a Sunday school class or youth group meeting, at the beginning of a new week, or during a meal. A blessing does not need to be attached to a special event, but a blessing will make an ordinary event special.

Jesus the Compassionate Priest

The Book of Hebrews is devoted to showing the ways in which Jesus functions as our perfect high priest. First, he intercedes for his people. Intercession requires compassion, and in order for a priest to have compassion for the people, that priest must experience the struggle of resisting sin. Jesus did this by becoming human. He is able to sympathize with the weaknesses of the people he serves (Hebrews 4:15), dealing gently with those who are ignorant or going astray (5:2) because he endured temptation without sinning. Jesus is qualified to plead our cases before the Father and has "entered heaven itself, now to appear for us in God's presence" (9:24). Second, his service to God motivated others to praise and worship (Luke 19:37-38). "Through Jesus, therefore, let us continually offer to God a sacrifice of praise—the fruit of lips that confess his name" (Hebrews 13:15). Third, Jesus led people in sacrifice and accepted their offerings. Sitting at the home of Simon the Leper, Jesus received the beautiful offering of perfume poured out on his head (Mark 14:3). He also led people in sacrifice by offering his life for the world. Finally, Jesus blessed the people in the sermon on the mountain (Matthew 5:3-11); he blessed Peter for his confession of faith (Matthew 16:17); and he blessed those who wash their robes (Revelation 22:14) to be pure like the high priest who calls them. In all these ways Jesus helped people re-connect with their God.

Jesus Brought People to God

Jesus performed the ultimate act of priestly responsibility by doing for us what former priests were unable to do: bring people fully to God. He did this through his once-and-final sacrifice of himself on the cross. As an inimitable juxtaposition of both priest and sacrifice, he offered himself to pay for the people's sins. At the moment Jesus gave up his spirit, the curtain in the Temple was torn in two (Matthew 27:51). Not from bottom to top as if a human defiled the Temple. It was torn from top to bottom by the One with the authority to invite humanity into the presence of the divine. In the past, the Temple curtain had separated the people from God. Only the high priest could enter the Holy of Holies, and he could go only once a year. In sacrificial love and duty, Jesus ripped away the curtain between God and his people. Therefore, "we have confidence to enter the Most Holy Place by the blood of Jesus, by a new and living way opened for us through the curtain, that is, his body" (Hebrews 10:19-20).

In the past, the barrier of ritual prevented anyone from approaching God whenever he or she chose. For even a priest to approach God without proper preparation would have resulted in death (Leviticus 16:2). Now we may approach the throne of grace with confidence and receive both mercy and grace to help us in our time of need (Hebrews 4:16).

In the past, the barrier of tribe prevented one from approaching God. Only the Levites were permitted to become priests and enter God's presence. But Jesus, a descendant of Judah, has made us all "a royal priesthood" (1 Peter 2:9).

In the past, the barrier of nationality prevented people from approaching God. That has now been removed, because "in Christ there is neither Jew nor Greek" (Galatians 3:28).

In the past, the barrier of gender prevented some from approaching God. Only males could become priests and females were less valued. Now "there is neither . . . male nor female . . . for [we] are all one in Christ Jesus" (Galatians 3:28).

In the past, the barrier of imperfection prevented people from approaching God. Even priests with disease, disfigurement, or any other physical ailment were not allowed to approach the curtain or the altar of God (Leviticus 21:17-23). But Jesus welcomed the lame, the blind, and the sick saying, "I have compassion for these people" (Matthew 15:31-32).

Jesus' death on the cross has eliminated every obstacle to intimacy with God . "Now in Christ Jesus you who once were far away have been brought near through the blood of Christ. For he himself is our peace, who has . . . destroyed the barrier, the dividing wall of hostility" that kept us from God. (Ephesians 2:13-14). As priests we must remind youth that God has removed these barriers.

The Temptation of Priests

As Moses lingered on the Sinai mountain, speaking with God, the people became restless. They wanted the assurance that God was leading them, so they enlisted Aaron's help. Aaron took the people's gold jewelry and fashioned it into a calf idol (Exodus 32:2-4). Whereas priests are supposed to accept the people's offerings and give them to God, Aaron took the people's offerings and made them into a false god. (Ironically, the gold they wore became the god they worshiped. Many people today are tempted to do the same.)

One of the greatest temptations that priests will face is the temptation to create idols for the people. Priests may be tempted to take the people from God to another, often more visible object of worship. Some teens fall into the trap of worshiping religious duties. Others put their trust in financial prosperity. Still others are deceived and claim allegiance to the priest (that is, whomever is playing the priestly role that I have described). When this happens, the teens replace their first love, God, with something of lesser, finite value that competes for the devotion that God deserves.

Part of the tragedy in the parable of the Good Samaritan is that, although priests are to represent the people, feel compassion for the suffering of others, and help others move closer to God, the priest and the Levite in the story avoided the beaten man by passing by on the other side. They forsook their identity. In one moment they denied the very purpose of their role and compromised their integrity.

Today's priests will function most effectively when they serve in the tradition of their early predecessors, who guarded the purpose of their profession. The first priests guarded this purpose in part through the adornment of their attire. The names of the twelve tribes of Israel were written on the breastplate, over the priest's heart. On his head, the gold plate of the priest's turban bore the words "HOLY TO THE LORD" (Exodus 28:36). Like an adhesive connecting two dissimilar entities, priests always carried with them a concern for sinful people and a respect for their holy God. May we honor this calling as God's royal priesthood:

> May the Lord answer you when you are in distress;
>   may the name of the God of Jacob protect you.
> May he send you help from the sanctuary
>   and grant you support from Zion. . . .
> May he give you the desires of your heart
>   and make all your plans succeed. (Psalm 20:1-2, 4)

Reflection

1. What groups of teens need someone to speak for them? Whose voice is not being heard in your church?

2. How does youth ministry help teens bring offerings to God? How does the church help teens make sacrifices?

3. How does youth ministry help teens worship?

4. What special blessing do the teens in your life need to receive? What opportunities for blessing do you have in your ministry?

Note

Trent, John and Gary Smalley. 2004. *The blessing: Giving the gift of unconditional love and acceptance.* Nashville, TN: Thomas Nelson.

UNIT 4

Focus of Relationships

Spiritual Friends and Equipping Recruiters

Genuine relationships are something many people lack but desperately crave. Teens are no exception. In one study almost forty percent of teens attending US churches said they do not have even one adult they can turn to for support, advice, and help (Smith 2005, 60), despite the fact that this is something a majority of them want. As Chap Clark reports, "Today's adolescents are, as a lot, indescribably lonely" (Clark 2004, 69). Their abandonment by adults has left them lost, fending for themselves (Yaconelli 2003, 95). "They are a tribe apart, remote, mysterious, vaguely threatening" (Hersch 1998, 14). The segregation of youth is not a trend the church should perpetuate or permit. Teens need mature spiritual friends who will love and guide them through the tumultuous years of adolescence. The youth pastor is integral to this process, but she must not attempt it alone.

To spend time solely with youth may send a message to the rest of the congregation that the youth pastor is the hired hand, or worse, surrogate parent, whose job is to take care of the teens in the church. Multiple adults, who have been recruited and equipped to serve with youth in ministry, are needed to build up the youth in the body of Christ. A youth minister who invests in adults by teaching them to minister to teens, will multiply his ministry. But the youth minister must model the type of ministry that he teaches to others. A minister cannot effectively model ministry to youth if he does not have relationships with youth. He must be a spiritual friend to teens while also recruiting and equipping adults.

Youth pastors need to balance the time they spend with teens and adults. Doug Fields suggests spending "50% of your relational time with your adult volunteer leaders and 50% of your time with students" (Fields 2002, 86). Alvin Reid claims, "Effective youth ministers . . . spend perhaps a third of the time with the students, a third of the time with parents and other significant adults, and a third of the time with all of them together" (Reid 2004, 154). This tension is probably best evidenced in Jesus' life by his balance of time spent with the crowds and time spent with his disciples. Often the two groups were together as the disciples learned to minister to the crowds by watching Jesus.

The youth minister is a bridge spanning the chasm created by the segregation of generations in the church and must model intergenerational connectivity through her relationships with people of all ages in the church. This occurs as the youth pastor invests time in relationships with adults as well as with teens.

Reflection

1. How has your church, either implicitly or explicitly, conveyed their expectations about the youth pastor's relational time?

2. What expectations do these groups have about how the youth pastor should invest time in his relationships?
    - church leadership
    - parents
    - teens

3. What are the advantages and disadvantages when a youth pastor spends too large an amount of time with adults? With teens?

Notes

Fields, Doug. 2002. *Your first two years in youth ministry*. Grand Rapids, MI: Zondervan/Youth Specialties.

Reid, Alvin L. 2004. *Raising the bar: Ministry to youth in the new millennium*. Grand Rapids, MI: Kregel.

Smith, Christian. 2005. *Soul searching: The religious and spiritual lives of American teenagers*. New York: Oxford University Press.

Clark, Chap. 2004. *Hurt: Inside the world of today's teenagers*. Grand Rapids, MI: Baker.

Hersch, Patricia. 1998. *A tribe apart*. New York: Ballantine.

Yaconelli, Mike. 2003. *The core realities of youth ministry*. Grand Rapids, MI: Youth Specialties/Zondervan, 94, 95.

CHAPTER EIGHT

Spiritual Friend

I met Will on the first day of my first youth ministry position after graduating from seminary. When I got to my office I had a message from him. He said that my name was listed in the city files as a community partner willing to assist teens with community service. (To this day I have no idea how my name got on that list.) Not knowing what to make of this information, I agreed to let him serve at the church building to get the hours he needed. But I told him I was going to do the work with him. Over the next few weeks we vacuumed classrooms, took out trash, replaced ceiling tiles, and did various other jobs. You learn a lot about a person when you work together. One of the things I learned was that his middle name was Joseph. When I asked him if he knew who Joseph was in the Bible he said "No." So we started reading Genesis together, and I gave him community service hours as he read, figuring that it was character formation, something that the city was also interested in.

Will had walked a rough road of drugs, alcohol, and failed relationships during his teen years. When I asked him why he lived the way he did, he said that when he is at a party no one judges him. They all accept him just the way he is, which was something he really valued. When I finally invited him to church he was surprised to find that people did not mind his tattoos or piercings. What Will experienced at church was another group of people who accepted him. The church loved him and supported the good decisions he had made but went further by affirming something else that was latent in him. We told Will that he could become a man after God's own heart. Although he bounced back and forth between two worlds, he kept coming back. He kept coming back because, by his own admission, in the church he had found true friends.

Many youth face a harsh reality in which they are left to themselves in isolation with no one to guide, counsel, or befriend them except for peers who themselves are estranged from adults. This presents an opportunity for youth ministry. The church should be a place where the generations interact and where it can be said, unquestionably, that Christian adults care for their young. The church should be one place where youth can find a spiritual friend.

Spiritual Friendships

The friendship between Jonathan and David illustrates what it means for friends to love each other, include God in the friendship, serve each other, share resources, protect each other, speak openly, commit to each other wholeheartedly, and endure together those factors that threaten to divide relationships.

Love as We Love Ourselves

The first thing that the Bible says about Jonathan's relationship with David is that the two friends were one in spirit and that Jonathan loved David "as himself" (1 Samuel 18:1). This phrase is repeated two other times to describe Jonathan's love for David (1 Samuel 18:3; 20:17). Jonathan and David modeled what it means to fulfill the second greatest commandment long before Jesus emphasized its importance.

Include God

While spiritual friends love each other as they love themselves, the one distinguishing characteristic of spiritual friends is their inclusion of God as a third party in the relationship. David reminded Jonathan on two occasions that God served as the notary for the relationship by stating, "for you have brought [me] into a covenant with you before the LORD" (1 Samuel 20:8), and "remember, the LORD is witness between you and me forever" (20:23). We know that Jonathan viewed God's role in a similar way because, when the two parted for the last time, Jonathan declared, "We have sworn friendship with each other in the name of the LORD, saying, 'The LORD is witness between you and me, and between your descendants and my descendants forever' " (20:42). Without God their relationship was invalid and their friendship was based on mere words. In the same way, without the inclusion of God, our friendship with an adolescent is little more than a benevolent enterprise. When we permit God to permeate our relationships, we set the stage for a spiritual friendship.

Serve One Another

The love that true spiritual friends have for each other is more than just words or ideas; it is shown in actions. When Jonathan first learned of his father Saul's plot to kill his friend, he said to David, "Whatever you want me to do, I'll do for you" (1 Samuel 20:4). This might not appear significant until we recall two important details. First, there was a significant age difference between David and Jonathan. When David fought Goliath he was a small boy who was unable to carry an adult's armor. By that time, Jonathan already had his own armorbearer and had successfully attacked the Philistines on several occasions (1 Samuel 13:3; 14:1). Second, Jonathan was the son of the king. As the prince of Israel, Jonathan did not need to submit to anyone; but he pledged loyalty to David, the true future king. Despite Jonathan's right to lord it over David, he chose to serve him.

In the same way, most of us do not need to befriend youth to find fulfillment as adults. There are other things we could be doing, but we choose to humble ourselves and become the servants of those who will inherit adulthood, with all its responsibilities, challenges, and rewards. Like David, our youth will become something else one day. Some will be moms or dads, politicians or military personnel, artists or athletes. But regardless of what a youth may become, adult friends of young people find in them something of value today. When Jonathan first befriended David he did not know that his young friend would one day become the king. What he did know was David's passion for God and his desire to serve.

It is equally striking that David, knowing he would become king, chose to submit to Jonathan. He went so far as to call himself Jonathan's servant (1 Samuel 20:8), and bowed down before him "three times, with his face to the ground" (20:41). This mutuality is a distinguishing characteristic of true friendships. When only one person in a relationship submits, the result is slavery or another form of dysfunctional dependence. In spiritual friendships one person may be more powerful than the other, but the powerful person chooses to serve the less powerful.

Share Resources

In a curious move toward the beginning of their friendship, Jonathan gave David his robe, his tunic, his bow, his belt, and most surprisingly, his sword (1 Samuel 18:4). What was intended as an expression of fidelity actually served as a portent of things to come. The prince's sword exchanged hands and became the sword of the king. In the same way, we also share resources with the youth we befriend. Among these are our own precious memories from the past, our experiences in the present, and our dreams for the future. We lay ourselves open before youth in appropriate ways to reveal both the shame of our broken humanity and the glory of Christ in us. That transparency serves to teach our youth the anatomy of a Christian adult and helps them along in their own journey.

Protect Each Other

Jonathan had a difficult day when he learned that his father Saul wanted David dead. As David broke the news Jonathan retorted, "Never! . . . It's not so!" (1 Samuel 20:2). To make matters worse, David told Jonathan that Jonathan could kill him if David was in fact guilty of any crime. Once again, Jonathan exclaimed, "Never!" (20:9), in denial that his father would have any evil plans for David's demise. In response to these allegations, Jonathan participated in a secret scheme to discover the true threat to David's life. They agreed that Jonathan would inform David of impending harm so that David could flee. Fully willing to endure the consequences of a curse, Jonathan declared, "May the LORD deal with me, be it ever so severely, if I do not let you know [Saul's plans] and send you away safely" (20:13). He was zealous for the protection of his friend and risked his own safety to help David.

It is somewhat misguided to believe that youth ministry can protect youth from all threats to their spiritual health. While youth do need some forms of spiritual protection, a defensive posture that retracts from the world is not always healthy given that God's kingdom is advancing (Matthew 11:12; 16:18). What we can protect is the reputation, dignity, and worth of our youth in the eyes of the church. Paul was aware that Timothy might be belittled because of his age and challenged him to let his life testify to his value (1 Timothy 4:12). Our friendship with youth can help protect them from the disparagement of older adults who decry a youth's ability to contribute anything meaningful until she is older.

Speak Openly

Another characteristic of spiritual friendships is their commitment to confidentiality. Friends speak openly to each other about matters that should not be discussed elsewhere. As Jonathan listened to David explain Saul's hatred for David, he said, "If I had the least inkling that my father was determined to harm you, wouldn't I tell you?" (1 Samuel 20:9). In essence, Jonathan affirmed that he and David had made a commitment to openness in their communication. They could trust each other with information that others could not know.

Friendship means telling the truth and speaking honestly about who we really are and how we truly feel. It means speaking boldly, even when doing so may not be convenient. We really have nothing to hide among friends because they know us better than anyone else and still love us. Teens crave that sort of assurance. They want to know that someone could know everything about them and still love them. That is the satisfaction many of us find in marriage, but it can be true of other friendships as well, as long as both parties have an undying commitment to the relationship.

Commit to the Relationship

When David killed Goliath and Jonathan observed David's commitment to God, Jonathan made a covenant of friendship with David (1 Samuel 18:3) that was later ratified (20:42). Fearing that his father intended harm to David, Jonathan agreed to help David escape Saul's wrath. At this point Jonathan extended his friendship covenant beyond David to include David's household and descendants. As they discussed the plan to help David escape, Jonathan's one request was this: "Show me unfailing kindness like that of the Lord as long as I live" (20:14). David willingly responded by reaffirming his love for Jonathan. This followed the commitment that David had already made to Jonathan, when David had pleaded, "Show kindness to your servant, for you have brought him into a covenant with you before the Lord" (20:8). These two friends were not thinking in terms of seasons or years. They were thinking about a lifetime of loyalty to each another. That sort of friendship will endure many tests and trials.

A freshman in high school once told me that he knew with certainty that I would leave the church for another ministry position before he left the church as a graduate. He had learned not to trust adults because adults, in his mind, were people who broke promises and failed to uphold commitments. He wanted proof that adults would stay in his life, but he would not believe it until he saw it. We can promise teens that we will stay in their lives, but we must back this promise with a willingness to endure opposition together.

Endure Opposition

Spiritual friendships will face opposition. Whenever two people who are one in spirit share a bond of trust, others will attempt to divide them. Saul became belligerent at Jonathan's defiant loyalty to David and cursed him by saying, "You son of a perverse and rebellious woman! Don't I know that you have sided with the son of Jesse to your own shame and to the shame of the mother who bore you? As long as the son of Jesse lives on this earth, neither you nor your kingdom will be established. Now send and bring him to me, for he must die!" (1 Samuel 20:30-31). When Jonathan protested, saying that David had done nothing wrong, Saul treated his own son as he had treated David and hurled a spear at him to kill him (20:32-33). Saul hated his son as he hated his enemy, but Jonathan loved David "as he loved himself" (20:17). Jonathan's life testifies that "there is a friend who sticks closer than a brother" (Proverbs 18:24) and sometimes even a father.

David and Jonathan's friendship entered a new phase the day Saul threw his spear at Jonathan and Jonathan shot his arrows toward David. One was a sign of anger and the other a signal of love. Because of Saul, the two friends could no longer be together as they had been; so they kissed each other and wept together before David departed (1 Samuel 20:41).

Sometimes the opposition we face in friendships with youth results in suffering. Other times it demands sacrifice. Youth pastors continually subject themselves to jealousy from others, belittling, or ridicule by choosing to love teens and serve in a profession that is often misunderstood or disrespected. Sometimes, an adult leader will wrestle with doubts about her profession that arise when she runs into a former classmate from college who has a house, car, and bank account that she will never have. When we risk becoming distracted by such things, we can focus on a model of spiritual friendship that will give us a healthy understanding of ministry and help us put things into perspective: the example of Jesus.

Our Friend Jesus

Jesus' commitment to his friendship with humanity is startling. First, he embodied the command to love others as he loved himself. When Paul admonished the Philippians to look not only to their own interests but also to the interests of others, he offered the life of Jesus as an illustration: "Your attitude should be the same as that of Christ Jesus: Who, being in very nature God, did not consider equality with God something to be grasped, but made himself nothing" (Philippians 2:5-6). Second, Jesus always kept God at the center of his friendships. He claimed that anyone who had seen him had also seen the Father (John 14:9), and he prayed that the believers who followed would be united just as Jesus and God the Father were united (John 17:23). Third, Jesus served his friends. "The Son of Man did not come to be served, but to serve, and to give his life" (Matthew 20:28). He demonstrated this service poignantly one night when he rose from the evening meal and washed his disciples' feet (John 13:2-17). Fourth, Jesus shared resources with his friends. Among these were God's words and his insight into what was to come. Like the father in the parable of two sons, Jesus says to his friends, "everything I have is yours"

(Luke 15:31). Fifth, Jesus was zealous for the protection of those he loved. Like a mother hen who gathers her chicks under her wing (Luke 13:34) and like a shepherd who holds on tightly to a sheep in danger (John 10:27-28), Jesus clings to those who are his. Next, Jesus spoke openly with his friends. Jesus made known his intentions to his disciples (John 15:15) and noted that this exchange of knowledge made them friends. Jesus also demonstrated friendship through his commitment to relationships, a commitment that endures, as he promised, to the very end of the age (Matthew 28:20). Finally, Jesus' friendship was strong enough to endure any opposition this world or the spiritual forces of evil could muster. Before his death Jesus explained, "Greater love has no one than this, that he lay down his life for his friends" (John 15:13). He then did exactly that as he went to the cross because of his love for us.

The pressing issue for us is probably not whether we believe Jesus is a reliable friend. That seems to be an easily acceptable claim. The real question is whether we will be friends to Jesus. Are we zealous to protect our friend's reputation? Do we demonstrate a willingness to serve him? Have we given over all of our resources for Jesus to use? Are we committed to the relationship, even in the face of the fiercest opposition? Once we have considered our own relationship with Jesus, we can teach youth that the invitation to discipleship is interrogative: Are you willing to be Jesus' friend?

What Spiritual Friendship Is Not

Before we go any farther, it might be helpful to consider what spiritual friendship is not. The goal of friendship with youth should never be to become as much like teens as possible. Instead, one objective of youth ministry should be to know teens and love them in their culture, helping them mature in their faith and "attain to the whole measure of the fullness of Christ" (Ephesians 4:13). "One sign of healthy adult leadership in youth ministry is the ability to be one with youth without becoming one of them. . . . These missionaries know . . . how and when to say, unapolegetically 'You're 14. I'm not' " (Dean and Foster 1998, 32). Too many Christian adults mistakenly believe that, in order to serve Christ among youth, they have to sacrifice maturity. Doug Fields has unequivocally advised, "Don't do what so many adults do when they want kids to like them and be impressed by them . . . act like teenagers!" (Fields 2002, 289). Teens do not want someone to show them what it looks like for an adult to act like a teen. They want to know how to navigate the transition to adulthood. This should be our focus. If for no other reason, "far too many adults look foolish trying to imitate adolescents" (Jackson 2000, 32).

In a similar way, being a spiritual friend to teens does not mean entertaining kids to the glory of God or keeping teens busy so that they do not sin. Instead, it is about equipping them with the faith, maturity, and strength to face—with God's help—life's struggles. Spiritual friendship with young people involves incarnational living in which we embody God's presence in the lives of youth and allow them to encounter God in Christian community. Two men in Gunnison, Colorado, have figured this out. Every Wednesday during the school year you will find Cliff and Kent at Webster Hall, the old Gunnison Community Center. They go there to host a lunch with an open invitation to any boy of high school age in the city. This weekly ritual costs Cliff several hundred dollars per meal, but he finds it to be a solid investment. Each week the boys herd in like cattle to feed because they know a good deal when they see one: free lunch and a good time with two hosts who care about them. These men not only cook the food, they offer a special form of friendship that the boys crave. It is not so much about listening to problems or sitting through counseling sessions. You are more likely to find these men telling a great story, giving a slap on the back, or holding the boys they serve to a higher standard. One year their lunchtime theme was "What does it take to be a Christian man?" and the emphasis was on service, so they all decided to do something during the lunch hour for other people. Their idea has since become an annual event. Once a year they invite all the high school age girls of the town to lunch and the boys serve them a meal. The recipe for successful ministry in this context is a touch of creativity, an ounce of courage, and a dollop of friendship.

Youth need adults like this who are brave enough to enter their world. Sometimes friendship with youth means just being aware of things in their lives. One youth minister spent the first five years of his ministry without a television but kept up with television shows through magazine and Internet reviews. That research paid off when conversations with teens included references to popular shows. Sometimes the best approach to friendship with teens is to simply be present among them, do a lot of listening, and, only after hearing what is said, share personal opinions and interests.

Offering Friendship to Youth

An advertisement for a national youth ministry conference several years ago showed an adult and a teen sitting at a table. The caption read, "Today, Alicia told you she thinks she is ready to accept Christ, her boyfriend is pressuring her to have sex, and she hates the way she looks. Pick one. Are you ready?" A few months after I saw that advertisement I was on a retreat with some high school students. During free time a girl sat down across from me to talk about how she was considering becoming a missionary, how she had just learned that her dad was having an affair on business trips, and how she wanted her boyfriend to stop dragging her down morally. My first thought was, "I wish I had attended that conference!" Our teens need Christian adults to be their friends. They need these friends to serve as spiritual directors and counselors for them. They need people to pray with them and invite God to be a part of the solution to their problems.

I recently asked Matt Wallace to explain the unique form of youth ministry he and his wife are involved with. These two work with Dry Bones, a ministry to homeless youth in Denver. What follows is his response to the question, "What have you found to be an effective way to reach youth?"

> The only thing that works in our ministry is love. We build meaningful and genuine relationships with the street kids. We try to live Christ always and never preach at the kids. The supernatural love of Christ is powerful and life-changing. These young people have typically never experienced any sort of genuine love in their lives. When real love slams into their life it's like seeing in color for the first time—it's amazing, there's clarity, and it's extremely scary. . . . We look for creative ways to heap value on these kids, like throwing them birthday parties, remembering and asking them about something that they told us weeks ago, visiting them in jail, raving over their new poem, or taking them into a real coffee shop as paying customers that they would normally be kicked out of. We view the street kids not as a target to evangelize, but

as an extremely valuable missing treasure. Everything we do has to demonstrate this value.

We have experienced that most kids belong long before they believe, so we try to provide a place for belonging. We rent out a pool hall once a week, share meals together, take kids to movies, church, and the zoo. It is also important for us to go to where the kids are. We hang out where they hang out. We call it "hang-out-reach."

We try not to create an "us/them" atmosphere, but rather an "us" environment. We're all in this journey together. It is vital that we keep an attitude of "I have just as much to learn from you as you might learn from me.". . . . The "service" we specialize in is friendship.

The National Study of Youth and Religion found that, when US adolescents ages 13 to 17 were asked about their experience talking with an adult youth minister or religious youth leader about a personal question or problem, the teens had overwhelmingly positive responses. While it is tragic that 81 percent of US teens have not had such a conversation, the 19 percent who have had one said that it was a good experience (Smith 2005, 64). The challenge for adults is to realize that an open-door policy is not sufficient to instigate these types of conversations. Adults must pursue relationships with teens where they are.

Donny was an only child. He was very intelligent and spent the better part of his junior and senior years of high school taking college courses to get a head start on his future. By his own admission he had only one or two close friends in the youth ministry. Attempting to befriend Donny, I called him regularly, invited him to join me in ministry tasks, served on his Eagle Scout review board, and saw movies with him. On one occasion I asked him if he considered me a friend. His reply was, "Can a teen be friends with the youth minister?" He was hesitant to view our relationship as something more than professional. His reply reminded me that some teens might resist expressions of friendship with youth pastors, being distrustful of our motivation. When I asked Donny what it would take for him to call our relationship a friendship, he said, "We would have to spend more time together." That seems to be the secret. Teens want and need caring adults to spent significant time with them. Teens also want this from one another.

Teens want someone courageous enough to show up in their world and support them. They want someone to cheer for them and applaud the ways in which they express themselves, use their gifts, and succeed. They want to be challenged and they want to be loved. If the church cannot provide such relationships, teens will seek them elsewhere. Such relationships require us to go where the teens are. Being a friend to teens means finding commonalities with those young persons whom other adults have despised or ignored. We can choose to connect with those who most need our friendship, thereby nudging them closer to friendship with God, or we can take the easier route of loving those who are like us. Jesus was known as the friend of tax collectors and sinners. How will we be known?

Reflection

1. When you were a teen, what did the adults in your life do that made an impact on you? Who modeled spiritual friendship for you? Were they parents, teachers, church leaders, others?

2. In what ways can an adult worker be a friend to teens in your ministry?

3. How did Jesus model friendship in ministry?

4. What are some barriers to being a spiritual friend to teens in your youth ministry? Who or what might stand in the way of your efforts to be a friend to youth?

Notes

Dean, Kenda Creasy and Ron Foster. 1998. *The Godbearing life: The art of soul tending for youth ministry.* Nashville: Upper Room Books.

Fields, Doug. 2002. *Your first two years in youth ministry: A personal and practical guide to starting right.* Grand Rapids, MI: Zondervan/Youth Specialties.

Jackson, Allen. 2000. Does the church need youth ministry? *American Baptist Quarterly.* March. 24 (1): 22-44.

Smith, Christian. 2005. *Soul searching: The religious and spiritual lives of American teenagers.* Oxford, England: Oxford University Press.

CHAPTER NINE
Equipping Recruiter

Larry James is President and CEO for Central Dallas Ministries (CDM), a human and community development corporation with a focus on economic and social justice that works in inner city Dallas (www.larryjamesurbandaily.blogspot.com). When he began at CDM, Larry spent his time interviewing low-income guests of the organization's food pantry. One day he found himself facing three Hispanic mothers and their children. Their limited English and Larry's minimal Spanish resulted in a communication struggle that kept these families from receiving the service they needed. As frustrations swelled, an older woman who had already been interviewed and assisted walked by. Larry stopped her to ask a question that had the power to change the culture and philosophy of CDM from that day forward. He simply asked, "Can you help me?" The woman gladly translated the conversation so that the families were able to receive assistance. As they were all leaving, the older woman offered to come back the following day to help again, an offer that was gladly accepted. She came back the next day for nine years. From that day on the people who came through the doors of CDM were encouraged to talk not only about their needs, but also about their assets. CDM invites every person whom they assist to return some form of service to the community as a volunteer.

In the same way, Christian adults have the potential to become valuable assets to youth ministry. Parents of teens in particular may come with their own concept of how youth ministry can help their children, but they are also indispensable resources in the spiritual development of their own teens and the other youth in the ministry. The one question we should learn to ask of parents and other adults is "Can you help me?"

Recruiting and Equipping

I went to lunch one day with the parent of a teen. This parent was a good friend and had offered wise advice in the past, so I took the opportunity to inquire about something that was on my mind. I asked him, "What do you expect of me as your teen's youth minister?" I was a little shocked when he replied, "Not as much as you think." It took a moment for me to understand what he meant, but I finally understood that it was not an insult. It was a relief. As he explained himself, I realized that his theology of the youth pastor was remarkably different from that of many parents' on two accounts.

First, he saw the youth pastor as a recruiter of adult volunteers who join together as a team to work with youth. Instead of taking individual ownership of the ministry, the youth pastor has the opportunity to enlist a cohort of adult volunteers to be partners in ministry. We need to learn again the wisdom of Jethro, Moses' father-in-law. When Jethro saw how Moses spent his time, sitting as the judge for the people from morning till evening, he rebuked Moses by saying, "What you are doing is not good" (Exodus 18:17). Serving alone as a judge for a nation and serving alone as a youth leader for a group of teens produces the same result: "You will only wear yourself out. The work is too heavy for you; you cannot handle it alone" (Exodus 18:18).

Second, my friend spoke of the supporting role youth pastors should play in the lives of families. He and his wife were raising their children in a Christian home and were trying to help their kids mature spiritually. He considered the youth pastor's work supplemental to the work he and his wife were doing at home. Youth pastors are resources for parents as well as partners who work with parents toward the common goal of their teens becoming Christian disciples. Some people think of the youth pastor as the primary spiritual guide for youth. Where there are Christian parents in the teen's life, this should not be the case.

If the first question youth ministers should ask other adults is, "Can you help me?" the second should be, "How can I help you?" The first is a matter of recruiting and the second a matter of equipping. These are inseparable components of connecting adults with youth. Just how we go about recruiting and equipping will differ from ministry to ministry, but the examples of several biblical leaders give us some guiding principles.

Description of Tasks

To begin, we need to know what we are asking volunteers to do. The one doing the calling must know what she is calling others to do. When individuals in the Bible were called into service, God usually informed them of the task to which they were called. God invited Moses to do the specific task of shepherding Israel. God called Jonah to preach to the city of Nineveh and called Paul to carry Jesus' name to the Gentiles. In each case God named a specific task that needed to be accomplished.

It is an indictment on youth ministry that at times we have invited Christian adults to join us without any specific instructions for what we expect them to do. We invite these adults into youth ministry service then treat them as many churches have treated teens, leaving them alone to fend for themselves. One way to prevent this is to create job descriptions for every role of adult service and to share these descriptions with volunteers. You might start by making a list of every ministry task the youth pastor has been doing and then reflecting on which of these tasks could be done by others. A youth minister should never be caught without an answer to the question, "What can I do to help?" Instead we can stay prepared by keeping a list of ways in which volunteers can serve, along with explanations of each role. We could even provide lists of roles based on how much time volunteers are able to commit to the ministry, whether that be thirty minutes a week, one hour, or more (Fields 2002, 186). Our volunteers deserve to know what we expect of them and to have some specific purpose for sacrificing time that could be spent somewhere else. Once we have identified what we need help with, we can begin to recruit and equip volunteers.

Prayer

Recruiting seems to work well when God's people talk with God about whom to recruit. In some cases, God has given direct instructions. For example, God approached Joshua and told him to select twelve men, one from each tribe, to pick up stones from the Jordan that would be used to build the memorial altar (Joshua 4:2). In other cases, people have sought counsel and guidance from God about whom to select. The eleven disciples who remained after Jesus' resurrection and ascension prayed that God would guide their selection of a new disciple, whether Barsabbas or Matthias. They prayed, "Show us which of these two you have chosen to take over this apostolic ministry" (Acts 1:24). Recruiting volunteers should not be one more task on a long list of duties. Instead, recruiting volunteers is a partnership we enter with God.

One day in the desert Moses was at his wits end. The Israelites' wailing had become like fingernails on a chalkboard to God, who was "exceedingly angry," and to Moses, who was "troubled" (Numbers 11:10). Moses joined in the complaining and cried out to God, saying, "Did I conceive all these people? Did I give them birth? Why do you tell me to carry them in my arms, as a nurse carries an infant, to the land you promised?" (11:12). Moses knew that these people were not his but God's and that God could not expect one person to carry them to Canaan. So God said to Moses, "Bring me seventy of Israel's elders who are known to you as leaders and officials among the people. . . . I will take of the Spirit that is on you and put the Spirit on them. They will help you carry the burden of the people so that you will not have to carry it alone" (11:16-17). Through this conversation, Moses and God negotiated a settlement that resulted in help for Moses and for the people of Israel.

In the same way, we join God in caring for God's children. It is a job that no one could possibly do alone. Together we seek out individuals who would be a good match for our ministry. As the disciples' actions testify, sometimes God has already selected the person or persons we are looking for. We just need the vision to see whom God has picked. One of the ways to do this is to look at what skills and qualities potential helpers possess.

Qualifications

Throughout Scripture we find requirements for specific roles and standards for positions of service. As we just saw, when Moses needed assistants, God told him to select seventy elders who were already leaders and officials among the people (Numbers 11:16). When Israel needed judges, Jethro told Moses to select capable, trustworthy men, who feared God and hated dishonest gain (Exodus

18:21). When Moses needed spies to explore the land of Canaan, God told him to choose people by the following criteria: one man from each tribe who is a leader among his people (Numbers 13:2). These men would have influence and persuasion among their people when the report came back. Likewise the criteria for apostleship after Judas's death were specific to the role: The person had to be one of the men who had been with the disciples from the days of John's baptism to the Ascension (Acts 1:21-22). Later in Acts, when a grievance arose regarding the distribution of food to widows, the apostles instructed the church to choose seven men who were known to be full of the Holy Spirit and wisdom (6:3). These may seem like odd criteria for a position dealing with food service and distribution, but poor judgment and irresponsible handling of resources had caused the conflict in the first place. The church needed people who were full of wisdom. The church later instituted requirements for the special roles of overseers (1 Timothy 3:1-7) and deacons (3:8-13). The task of Christian youth ministry is too important for us to settle for any warm body to fill a position of service. We need standards to guide our selection of those who work in our ministries. To determine these standards, we must reflect on the job that needs to be done, the skills required, and the giftedness of people.

The youth pastor does not have a monopoly on discernment in these matters. The testimony of others must be considered when we recruit volunteers. We see this at play in Scripture. The brothers at Lystra and Iconium spoke well of Timothy (Acts 16:2), which may have influenced Paul's decision to take the young disciple along on his journey. The Christians in these cities that Paul had visited saw something in Timothy before Paul realized his gifts. In the same way, we may learn of potential volunteers from the recommendations of others. At times we can enlist teens to help us find volunteers. They are usually willing to offer suggestions of people they admire and would like to help lead the ministry. Once we, or those around us, discern the right person for the job, the next step is to make contact and offer a personal invitation to ministry service.

Personal Invitation

When God's people were enslaved in Egypt, God did not send out an advertisement among the Hebrews for the open position of political leader and deliverer. Instead God went to a specific Hebrew refugee on a remote mountain. Too often we assume that broad-based pleas for volunteers will result in large numbers of respondents. What generally happens is one of two extreme results: the broad brush does not connect with anybody who feels a responsibility to act, or you receive a large number of volunteers who are unqualified for service.

The personal invitation is a powerful motivator when it comes to recruiting. When people know that you have prayed about this invitation and considered their individual gifts before approaching them, they are more likely to accept your invitation and more willing to help you find successors when they resign.

While recruiting can be an exacting responsibility unto itself, it is only half the battle in dealing with volunteers. Once you have recruited people, you must equip them for their service.

Equipping

It is not enough to match people with tasks. Youth ministers must ensure that volunteers have the resources to accomplish the task we have called them to. In other words, volunteers cannot just be recruited; they need to be equipped. After Moses had recruited his twelve spies to spy out the land of Canaan, he specified a route for them to take and a checklist of tasks that they were to accomplish (Numbers 13:17-20). He equipped the spies to fulfill their purpose. Sending servants with the tools they need to do the job was an important lesson that Moses may have learned from his own call to serve. When God first enlisted him to deliver Israel from Egypt, Moses protested by naming his deficiencies. God responded by equipping Moses with additional resources for the task: a staff that could become a snake, a hand that could become leprous, the promise that Nile water poured on the ground would become blood, and a spokesperson in the form of Moses' brother, Aaron (Exodus 4:1-17).

Youth pastors equip their adult volunteers by supplying them with resources and training them with skills for effective service. The resources we offer could include current information from research studies about adolescents, insights into youth culture, such as interpretations of their language, books and seminars on parenting, a guest speaker to offer encouragement, or stories of how we have handled difficult situations. We serve as resources by providing curriculum, audio and visual teaching aids, and any other supplies volunteers need to succeed in their roles. Sometimes we provide a valuable resource simply by encouraging communication among the volunteers about the lessons they have learned while serving.

In addition to offering resources, the youth pastor has a responsibility to train volunteers so that they can develop the skills they need to do tasks such as leading small groups, maintaining conversations with introverted teens who see themselves as outsiders, blessing teens, and backing a church van with a trailer. As we go about equipping, we must always remember the true source of all that we might offer and continually point adult volunteers back to God and the Bible as resources for their work. Paul reminded Timothy that the Scriptures are useful for "training in righteousness" so that people can be "equipped for every good work" (2 Timothy 3:16-17). Part of our equipping should focus on the personal spiritual development of adult volunteers in youth ministry. As we infuse healthy Christian adults into youth ministry, we increase the probability that the ministry will produce healthy Christian teens.

Ongoing Support

The final task in the process of working with volunteers is to continue supporting their work. As Moses served in the role God had recruited him for, he had access at any point to conversation with God. This access became helpful when Israel grumbled, became defiant, or wanted to stone their leader. In the same way, Paul supported his disciples Timothy and Titus with letters of encouragement. The support we offer might involve taking volunteers to lunch to ask about their experiences; continued coaching on what it means to be a teacher with youth; or taking all the youth volunteers to a professional sporting event each year for fellowship (as one youth minister I know has done).

Jesus, the Equipping Recruiter

The night before Jesus selected twelve of his disciples to become apostles, he went up on a mountainside to pray. Luke records that Jesus "spent the night praying to God" (Luke 6:12-13). This conversation may have informed his decision about whom to select. While there is no record of qualifications for the role of apostle, we do know that they each possessed a willingness to trust the one who had called them. Others whom Jesus called did not leave professions or families or future opportunities as readily as those whom Jesus named as his twelve apostles (Luke 9:59-62). Next, it appears that Jesus offered a personal invitation to each of these men. Mark says that Jesus called to him those he wanted, suggesting he was selective with the process (Mark 3:13). The description for the task came as these men were called: "Follow me," Jesus said, "and I will make you fishers of men" (Mark 1:17).

After recruiting his disciples, Jesus also equipped them for ministry. He trained them by sending them out in pairs to do mission work. He supplied them with resources by giving them the authority to drive out evil spirits and heal diseases (Matthew 10:1). As a promise of ongoing support, he told his disciples, "I am with you always, to the very end of the age" (Matthew 28:20) and gave them the Holy Spirit (Acts 2).

Barriers to Recruiting Volunteers

Recruiting volunteers for ministry will not always be easy, as there are several potential barriers to effective recruiting. We may discover that self-reliance inadvertently pushes away persons who would otherwise be willing to serve. Thinking that we have everything covered, potential volunteers may decide to work in another ministry where they feel needed.

We create another obstacle when we fail to communicate a compelling vision of why we need volunteer workers. Without a concept of how they can be useful in youth ministry, some adults just try to invest where they know they can see results.

A third barrier to effective recruiting is the simple fear of rejection. To avoid having to hear the terminal sound of the word "No," he refuses to ask anyone to do anything. The game of basketball illustrates the flaw in this sort of thinking: It is impossible for a player to score a basket if she does not shoot the ball. Few people make every shot they take in one game. Most will repeatedly fail; but when the ball does go through the net, they are inspired to shoot again. In the same way, some people whom we think are perfect for a specific role, for any number of reasons, decline our invitation. Instead of getting frustrated when this happens, we should see ourselves as being one person closer to discovering the right person for the job and shoot again.

Finally, the teens themselves can be an obstacle to enlisting qualified volunteers in youth ministry. One Wednesday night at our youth ministry meeting, a new volunteer joined us who happened to be the parent of a senior girl in the youth ministry. This mom had been recruited because of her skill in building relationships and initiating conversations with the teen girls. After the meeting the woman's daughter stormed over to me and defiantly declared that her mom would not be coming back to our Wednesday meetings. I asked her why, and she said, "Because I don't want her here!" I told the girl how valuable her mom had been in other areas of the youth ministry and that the other teen girls really benefited from her friendship. She would not move from her position, so I told her that she would have to work out the situation with her mom. After the two of them talked, the mom decided this was not a battle she wanted to fight; but she was not deterred. While she never came back on a Wednesday night, this mother volunteered in another area of youth ministry where her daughter was not involved.

Despite these obstacles and others, we need the resolve to continue pursuing volunteers. Without them, we face the danger of doing ministry alone.

The Danger of Doing Ministry Alone

We take a great risk when we fail to enlist others in service. "If you don't share your work load, you will damage the foundation of your ministry and quench the possibility of workers expressing their giftedness" (Fields 1998, 203). An essential task of the youth leader is to bridge the chasm between the generations by modeling connectivity with youth then bringing other adults into the ministry. Along the way, we can inspire these adults by helping them understand how they exhibit the roles described in this book. When we do this, the volunteer team becomes a collection of people with diverse gifts who function in various roles for the sake of youth. Unfortunately, this type of group does not always congeal. In one study, 40 percent of youth ministers who changed churches were cited as reasons a lack of adequate lay leadership for youth ministry and a lack of congregational support for the work of the youth pastor (Grenz 2002, 83). While these statistics may reflect unhealthy congregations, they may also reflect a failure on the part of youth pastors to recruit and equip volunteers. We may think that doing things ourselves will simplify our responsibilities and help us accomplish more at a higher level of quality, but it often does the exact opposite. Going it alone complicates our lives, forces us to do less, and hurts the quality of our work. If that were not enough, by failing to enlist volunteers in ministry we actually block others from using their gifts in God's service. That is not something I want to answer for when I stand before God. Our job is to "prepare God's people for works of service, so that the body of Christ may be built up until we all reach unity in the faith and . . . become mature, attaining to the whole measure of the fullness of Christ" (Ephesians 4:12). No one youth pastor can possibly tend to all of his teens' spiritual needs. Therefore, after attending to the pastor's personal relationship with God, the most essential professional task of a youth pastor is to recruit and equip Christian adults to be partners in youth ministry.

Reflection

1. What opportunities exist for the youth pastor to build relationships with and recruit adults in the church? If you are not recruiting effectively, what could you do differently?

2. Create a list of roles and qualifications for positions of service in your youth ministry. Who are the people who best match these criteria?

3. Which aspects of recruiting—describing the tasks to be done, prayer, setting qualifications, offering a personal invitation, equipping, and providing ongoing support—have you done well? Which have you done poorly?

Notes

Fields, Doug. 1998. *Purpose driven youth ministry*. Grand Rapids, MI: Zondervan.

Fields, Doug. 2002. *Your first two years in youth ministry: A personal and practical guide to starting right*. Grand Rapids, MI: Zondervan/Youth Specialties.

Grenz, Jonathan. 2002. Factors influencing vocational changes among youth ministers. *Journal of Youth Ministry*. 1(1): 73-88.

UNIT 5

Division of Responsibilities

Visionary Leaders and Faithful Teammates

To serve in youth ministry requires competencies common to many positions of church ministry. These skills include teaching (Chesnut 1975, 283), organization (Rowell 1981, 69), administration (Kuhne and Donaldson 1995, 151), and communication skills (Dearborn 1995, 7). As a generalist, the youth minister must know how to relate to people of different generations. The youth minister also must invest in relationships with organizational clusters such as elders, deacons, parents, and ministry volunteers while maintaining significant relationships with youth. In the strictest sense the youth pastor is a minister whose responsibilities include youth. As a generalist in ministry, the youth pastor is a faithful teammate with the responsibility of supporting the multiple ministries of the church.

In contrast, the youth minister is also a visionary leader: a specialist who looks toward what his ministry could become. Although the youth minister should have the skills of a generalist, she is often required to serve as a specialist with unique knowledge and competencies of specific subjects relevant to the field (Rahn 1996, 81). These include adolescent development, family relationships, youth culture, counseling, and adolescent spiritual formation.

Certain issues arise for the youth minister who is spread thin as a faithful teammate. This individual may be limited in the amount of time and attention he can offer to teens who desperately need relationships with adults who love them. Conversely, a youth ministry segregated from the rest of the church—the "one-eared Mickey Mouse" effect—is likewise a reflection of the youth minister's poor leadership (Cummings-Bond 1989, 76). As visionary leaders of youth ministry, some youth ministers have contributed to their ministry's disconnectedness in the church by their own lack of involvement with other ministries. Such isolation can lead to minister burnout, dilute the ministry's effectiveness in influencing the larger church, and prevent potential volunteers from knowing about the youth ministry.

Reflection

1. Does your church expect the youth pastor to be more of a specialist or more of a generalist?

2. What are the advantages and disadvantages of a youth leader being focused solely on the youth ministry? What are the advantages and disadvantages of a youth pastor being involved in multiple ministries of the church?

3. What education should be required for those serving as youth ministers, whether as generalists or specialists? Should this happen on the undergraduate or graduate level?

4. How can training and educational opportunities such as denominational certification programs and youth ministry conferences equip youth pastors as visionary leaders and faithful teammates?

Notes

Chesnut, Robert A. 1975. Internship year: Preparation for professional self-development. *Theological Education* 11 (Summer): 279-84.

Cummings-Bond, Stuart. 1989. The one-eared Mickey Mouse. *Youthworker*. 6 (Fall): 76.

Dearborn, Timothy A. 1995. Preparing new leaders for the church of the future: Transforming theological education through multi-institutional partnerships. *Transformation* 12 (4): 7-12.

Kuhne, Gary W., and Joe F. Donaldson. 1995. Balancing ministry and management: An exploratory study of pastor work activities. *Review of Religious Research* 37 (December): 147-63.

Rahn, Dave. 1996. What kind of education do youth ministers need? *Christian Education Journal*. 16 (3): 81-89.

Rowell, J. Cy. 1981. The skills, knowledge and tasks of the professional church educator. *Lexington Theological Quarterly* 16 (April): 68-75.

CHAPTER TEN

Visionary Leader

Kristi and Lori grew up as friends in Portland, Oregon, but attended college in Searcy, Arkansas. One spring break they went with a group to an inner-city church in Houston, Texas, called Impact, where they spent the week loving kids. Because of their experience on this trip, these two college students began dreaming about what a similar ministry might look like back home. Not knowing exactly what to do next, these women met regularly to pray and committed to spend five years investigating how to apply the lessons they learned from the Houston church in Portland. Over those next five years, life happened. Lori went to Africa, Kristi pursued a degree in counseling, they both got married, and the vision all but disappeared. Then Lori's brother, Lanny, and a friend named Ike began talking about planting a church. One night Kristi, Lori, Lanny, and Ike were all together sharing their visions for ministry and they realized it had been five years since the women had started praying about this very thing. Immediately, the group flew to Houston to learn everything possible from the ministers of the Impact church about the journey they were about to take.

In 2000, the Portland Urban Mission Project (PUMP) began as the four started a church in an ethnically diverse part of the city. Like Robert Raikes, who had looked on the street children of Gloucester, England, with compassion and had begun Sunday schools, these two women saw the children of their hometown and started the PUMP Summer Program. This program touches hundreds of kids during the summer by teaching them how to read, connecting them with caring adults, and educating them about choices and consequences. While the staff at PUMP continues to think about their future, they are living in the dream that two college students envisioned years earlier.

The Importance of Vision

The value of vision in leadership is hard to overstate. When leaders envision possibilities for the future of their ministries, they set priorities about what goals they will and will not pursue. Vision sets the stage for accomplishment, inspires people with encouragement and renewed purpose, and unifies others around a common goal.

Vision Precedes Accomplishment

We may understand the mission of the church and the purpose of youth ministry, but if we have no vision for how to accomplish this mission and purpose we will likely get lost along the way. When Moses sent the twelve spies to do complete military reconnaissance in the land of Canaan, they took forty days to inspect the quality of the land, the number and strength of the people, the structure of their cities, and the trees and fruit found there. Upon their return, they reported "[the land] does flow with milk and honey," but ten of the spies could not get past how small the people of Israel seemed compared to the formidable foes of Canaan. Ten of the spies saw the size of the people in Canaan while two of the spies saw the size of the God in Israel (Numbers 13:26–14:9).

Similar cases of distorted vision appear throughout the Bible. David's brothers saw an unbeatable giant while David saw a defiant, disrespectful Philistine who needed to be silenced (1 Samuel 17). Eleven disciples in a boat saw the wind and the waves, but Peter saw Jesus, and walked out toward him (Matthew 14:25-31). When Saul was converted, many in the early church saw him as a murderous threat to their lives; but Barnabas saw him as a new convert with a sincere testimony of transformation and welcomed him with hospitality (Acts 9:26-27).

The youth pastor who has a vision for the future is more likely to see that future realized than the youth pastor who cannot see past this Sunday. Regardless of the circumstances, youth pastors who are visionary leaders hold on to the hope that God will work through the church's youth ministry to engage teens with the gospel. Shirking fatalism and hopelessness, visionary leaders of youth ministries see a future that only God's power can accomplish. They see what youth can become and then work to make it happen. Although some visions are context-specific, here is this author's vision for the future of youth ministry in general:

> That the focus of youth ministry would be to help teens be the church in this culture, instead of using the culture to create a subset within the church.

> That youth would leave our ministries with a maturing faith in Jesus that expresses itself in service and a commitment to the church.

> That adults in churches would feel a responsibility to contribute to the faith development of the younger generation.

> That teens would see in the lives of the adults who work with them examples of people whose lives have been redeemed and transformed.

> That youth pastors would model Christian living in such a way that even more young men and women would be attracted to a life of ministry and service in Jesus' name.

> That those youth who do not enter professional ministry would find their place as ministers in their respective professions.

> That youth ministry would be seen by the rest of the church as the fulfillment of the great commission with an accessible audience during one of the most receptive stages of life.

Those types of visions are more likely to be accomplished if they are shared with other people who can see that future as well. Ultimately, the people of Israel could not see Joshua and Caleb's vision. They listened instead to the fear of the other ten spies. The result was forty wasted years when the people could have been enjoying the Promised Land. Had they only seen what Joshua and Caleb had seen they would have moved forward into Canaan. This is a second benefit of clear vision. When people see the vision, it inspires and motivates them toward the goal.

Vision Provides Encouragement

When Joram was king of Israel, the king of the rival nation of Aram looked for opportunities to attack Israel. The king of Aram continually set up camp at secret locations to ambush the Israelites, but the prophet Elisha would inform Joram before the Israelite army had reached the location. (See 2 Kings 6:8-10.) The king of Aram was livid that plans he made in secret were being shared with his enemy, so he sought out the one responsible. When he discovered that Elisha was to blame, he sent an army of chariots and horses by night to surround the city of Dothan where Elisha was staying. Elisha's servant awoke to this frightening scene and asked the prophet what they should do because it appeared as though they were already defeated. With reassurance Elisha said, "Those who are with us are more than those who are with them" (2 Kings 6:16). So that the servant could enjoy the perspective of the prophet, Elisha prayed that God would open his servant's eyes. God did open the eyes of the servant, who saw the hills all around them full of horses and chariots of fire. This vision changed everything.

The vision we have for our youth ministry changes everything. It affects how we spend our time, what trips we take, how much money we invest, and whom we enlist to join us. The hope of making the vision a reality inspires us to keep going, and any progress toward that end is encouraging. Vision assuages fears and renews hope. It reminds people why they do what they do and gives them the energy to continue on. Stephen drew energy from his vision immediately before his opponents stoned him. Looking up, he saw heaven open with Jesus standing at the right hand of God (Acts 7:55-56). That type of vision alters one's understanding of reality and provides one with the impetus to keep going. This may be the reason both Paul and the Hebrews writer encouraged others to look where Stephen was looking. "Let us fix our eyes on Jesus" (Hebrews 12:2), and "Set your hearts on things above, where Christ is seated at the right hand of God" (Colossians 3:1).

In 1820, a baby girl was born in Putnam County, New York. At six weeks old she was blinded by a sudden illness. Undeterred by her inability to see, she successfully memorized Scripture and became a teacher who enjoyed writing poetry, which she did prolifically. At the age of fifty-three she wrote the words that would appear on her gravestone years later: "Blessed assurance, Jesus is mine! O what a foretaste of glory divine!" Looking more closely at the words of the classic hymn, "Blessed Assurance," we get a glimpse of what Frances Jane Crosby could see: "Visions of rapture now burst on my sight . . . watching and waiting, looking above, filled with his goodness, lost in his love." Fanny Crosby may have been blind, but she had vision that has inspired the countless people who have sung that hymn, because she looked beyond what most of us see. When we see our Christian service in light of Jesus' victory, it gives us hope, courage, and the strength to continue.

Vision Promotes Unity

Vision not only lays the groundwork for accomplishment and propels people toward a goal, it also promotes unity among those who see it. When Nebuchadnezzar set up a gold image on the plain of Dura in Babylon, his herald commanded the people to bow down in worship or "be thrown into a blazing furnace" (Daniel 3:6). At the sound of music, all of the people did as they were told—except for three Jewish court officials. When confronted with an order to bow before the king's image, these three individuals united around the belief that a God without image or form should be the only God they worshiped. Shadrach, Meshach, and Abednego had never endured the flames of a fire, but they had the vision to declare to Nebuchadnezzar that God could and would save them (Daniel 3:17). Their vision cost them their jobs and got them thrown into a furnace. (History tells us that these things tend to happen to people who share their vision with those who simply cannot see.) Eventually Nebuchadnezzar, the king who needed an image to worship, became a believer when he saw a "son of the gods" in the fire and three men unscathed by the furnace (Daniel 3:25). When all was said and done, the king caught the vision of the three Jews and believed in their God.

When someone can communicate to others a picture of what the future might look like, it tends to have a unifying effect. When the vision itself involves unity, that effect is amplified. Peter had such a vision on the roof of Simon the Tanner's house (Acts 10:9-16).

Seeing animals lowered on a sheet and hearing a voice from heaven instructing him to eat those animals—some of which were unclean under Jewish dietary laws—he came to understand more about God's plan; and God's plan influenced his actions. He immediately went to Cornelius's house where he shared the good news of his vision with the Gentiles assembled there (Acts 10:17-43). God had something in mind that Peter needed to understand, namely, that the gospel of Jesus Christ was for Gentiles as well as Jews. The early church's subsequent successful mission to Gentiles throughout the Roman world began with a vision.

Like Peter, we need vision not only to see a future goal that we can aim for but also to see what God is doing and to join it. Too often we find ourselves in the place of Balaam, riding along unaware that the direction in which we are going displeases God. Balaam's donkey saw more of what God was doing than his rider did! When Balaam's eyes were eventually opened, he repented and changed direction. (See Numbers 22:22-35.) The same thing happened to Saul. The blinding light that left him without sight helped him see more clearly (Acts 9:3-8).

As with the other roles we have looked at, Jesus is our clearest example of a visionary leader.

Jesus, the Visionary Leader

Leadership is the relational process of influencing others toward a shared goal. Whether the leader needs to convince people of a goal's merit or the people already possess the motivation to accomplish the objective, leaders continually influence those who follow. This influence takes many forms. Some people respond to leaders who make forceful decrees, such as military leaders; others respond better to the gentle nudge of a tender shepherd. At times either may be appropriate. While leadership looks different in different settings, certain principles are always relevant to how leaders guide their groups. What follows is an eight-stage process for leading people that emerges from Jesus' life. This list, inspired in part by John Kotter's recommendations for leading change (Kotter 1996, 21), provides a framework for youth pastors as they function as visionary leaders of youth ministry.

Envision the Future

As ministry specialists, youth pastors have the opportunity to fully engage in youth ministry, leading, directing, and managing the people and assets involved. We have budgets, youth, opportunities, volunteers, and limitless possibilities with which to work. What are we doing with these resources? Whether we find ourselves with one teen or five hundred teens, we know that the master will return expecting to see what we have done with what was entrusted to us (Matthew 25:14-30). Discerning what God could do with your ministry takes vision. As you dream, remember that God can do more than we ask or imagine (Ephesians 3:20).

During Jesus' earthly ministry, he shared some visions for what the future could become. He described a day when true worshipers would worship in spirit and truth (John 4:23), a day when all of his followers would be united (17:21), a day when he would be lifted up so that all who believe in him would have eternal life (3:14-15), and a day when people would inhabit the house of God (14:2). His followers have embraced these visions because Jesus saw these things and shared them with others. And he communicated these visions with an urgency that made his message more poignant.

Establish Urgency

The first words from Jesus in Mark's Gospel capture the immediacy of his message: "The time has come. . . . The kingdom of God is near. Repent and believe the good news!" (Mark 1:15). Jesus came to proclaim the good news and would not settle for half-hearted commitments from his followers. Jesus said to a willing disciple who wanted to first bury his father, "Let the dead bury their own dead, but you go and proclaim the kingdom of God" (Luke 9:60). Apparently there are actions of eternal consequence that require our attention, even when day-to-day commitments scream for attention. This is the message of the parable of the rich man who wanted to take life easy, building bigger barns for himself. God said to him, "You fool! This very night your life will be demanded from you" (Luke 12:20).

As youth ministers, urgency is inherent in our message and ministry. On the day of the Columbine shooting in 1999, when it was

my neighborhood on the news, and teens from *my* youth group hud-
dled under desks in the school library, I realized that anything can
happen in a day; anything good and anything bad. You do not know
when a parent's job transfer, a car wreck, or a school shooting will
take away teens from your church's sphere of influence. Despite
any attempts to deny the passage of time, the clock continues tick-
ing on our window of opportunity to minister to teens. If we want
more than minimal results in the time we have, we will need help.

Enlist Support

Although Jesus single-handedly offered himself as a sacrifice for
the sins of the world, he depended on his disciples for almost every
other aspect of his ministry and counted on them to continue his
work in the world. He surrounded himself with a cohort of volunteers who provided financially for him (Luke 8:3), defended him
(Matthew 26:51), loved his family (John 19:26), and worked toward
the vision he had communicated after he left (Acts 1–2). Our ministries will not thrive and we will not survive without a band of
brothers and sisters who share our passion for youth ministry. For
this reason, recruiting others to join us is paramount among the
tasks of our profession. Part of this responsibility involves endlessly
communicating the vision and illustrating the roles that others can
play in making that vision a reality. It also requires us to model the
service that we expect from others.

Engage Yourself

While Jesus' ministry depended on the support of others, he did not
expect those around him to do everything while he sat by idly. He
fully engaged in the mission and thereby inspired those who worked
with him. Unlike leaders who bark commands from a safe distance,
Jesus got dirty with everyone else. The foot washing in John 13 is
a metaphor for his entire life. Getting up from the evening meal, he
voluntarily performed the pungent act of washing the disciples'
feet. Although he was both Rabbi and Lord, he set an example that
his followers would imitate. Jesus never asks his followers to do
anything he has not already done. In fact, his example was so thor-
ough that all we need to do is walk as Jesus did (1 John 2:6).

Youth ministers should model the commitment and sacrifices that they expect from other adults who are iinvolved in the youth ministry. It is inspiring to see a leader take the lowest place at a table or to refrain when another person wants to speak. These actions communicate clearly that a leader has a humility that testifies to his authenticity. Our leadership in youth ministry can be marked by self-promotion or it can be marked by service. Part of this service includes equipping those around us.

Equip Others

We have already seen from the Equipping Recruiter discussion that Jesus equipped his disciples with the Holy Spirit and the abilities to drive out evil spirits and heal diseases (Matthew 10:1). In addition to these skills, he gave them the opportunity to put their gifts to use by sending them on short-term mission experiences (10:5). The Son of God was unquestionably a better missionary than these recruits but he valued their inclusion; and, as a result, people were blessed.

In moments of weakness we may be tempted to withhold knowledge that sets us apart and gives us a competitive edge. Who does not enjoy being the resident expert on culture, teaching, and communicating with youth? While this information may benefit our reputations when we keep it in our possession, teens benefit when we give it away. By sharing what we have learned with parents and other adults we empower them to work more effectively with youth.

Encourage Supporters

After equipping his followers, Jesus encouraged them to continue in their work. When they felt alone his disciples heard the promise, "Remain in me, and I will remain in you" (John 15:4). When they felt discouraged they heard, "Do not let your hearts be troubled" (John 14:1), and when they felt encumbered by the weight of responsibility, he said, "Come to me, all you who are weary and burdened, and I will give you rest" (Matthew 11:28). Jesus lavished encouragement on those who had volunteered to work with him, knowing that they needed affirmation to continue serving.

People today are no different in this regard than Jesus' disciples. Youth ministry volunteers both need and deserve affirmation from the youth pastor. They often sacrifice time, money, and other opportunities to serve among youth who may not remember to be grateful. When the youth pastor also forgets to express gratitude and offer encouragement, the volunteers may get the impression that they are neither valued nor expected to remain in service very long. The reality is that they need encouragement because there will be instances that test the resolve of anyone involved in youth ministry.

Endure Opposition

Jesus knew that he would face opposition; his disciples knew that they would face opposition; and Jesus and his disciples foretold that we would face opposition as well. As Paul said, "Everyone who wants to live a godly life in Christ Jesus will be persecuted" (2 Timothy 3:12). Jesus endured the fierce and deadly opposition that he faced by resisting temptation, escaping attempts on his life, and finally passing through death back to life.

Leaders have always been opposed. Youth ministry leadership is no different. Some opposition can be prevented, but when a leader guides people toward a goal, there will inevitably be those who reject what the leader is doing or how he is doing it. Youth pastors receive criticism for not supporting specific camps or events that parents cherish, spending too much time away from the office, spending too much time in the office, not spending enough time with the junior high students, not having enough fun activities, not increasing the size of the group, inviting too many teens from the community who threaten the safety of others, planning too many activities that are expensive, and so on. Some of those criticisms are legitimate, but many are the result of ministerial myopia. Whenever someone enacts a kingdom-centered vision for youth ministry, some will be left scratching their heads and wondering what happened to the old way of doing things.

Evaluate Progress

Jesus was a proponent of evaluation and even provided criteria for the process. He was known to curse fig trees that did not produce figs (Matthew 21:19) and say things like "[God] cuts off every branch in me that bears no fruit" (John 15:2). If ministries are held to the same standard as fig trees and vine branches, we have some serious reflection to do. We should ask ourselves, "Are our youth being formed in the image of Christ?" "Do they demonstrate faithfulness to God after leaving this ministry?" and "How are they engaged in service, ministry, and missions?" For more specific evaluation standards, create questions based on your vision for ministry. After all we cannot measure progress if we do not consider what we are aiming for in the first place.

Youth Ministry Leadership

If leadership were as simple as working through a list of principles or responsibilities, more people would be great leaders. The truth is that leadership is about influence and that often involves working on several things at once. We may have a long-time volunteer to encourage while we enlist a new young couple to lead a Bible study. We may find ourselves enduring opposition about a change in retreat location while we envision new dreams for a mission trip. These needs arise, and the youth pastor must give them her attention and attend to them in a timely manner.

Thousands of years ago Solomon asked God for help with leadership. His prayer is still beneficial to youth pastors today. He prayed, "Give me wisdom and knowledge, that I may lead this people, for who is able to govern this great people of yours?" (2 Chronicles 1:10). As those entrusted with the souls of youth, may we seek wisdom and knowledge so that we can lead our people with vision.

Reflection

1. What aspects of Jesus' ministry required visionary leadership?

2. What leadership skills did Jesus demonstrate that you have found helpful in ministry?

3. What is your vision for youth ministry? How does your ministry, in practice, reflect this vision?

4. What hinders your ability to effectively lead in youth ministry?

Note

Kotter, John P. 1996. *Leading change*. Boston, MA: Harvard Business School Press.

CHAPTER ELEVEN
Faithful Teammate

Several years ago a church staff found itself in quite a predicament. Three of its five ministers were finishing seminary degrees, one was a recent staff addition, there were plans for one minister to retire, and the busiest season of this church's calendar was approaching. To top it all off, several staff members had conferences to attend. Everyone's greatest concern was finding a way to cover all the responsibilities of ministry during these few months.

Without a meeting or a master plan, the individuals involved, who knew each other's schedules, volunteered to take responsibility for ministries other than their own. The worship minister led worship with the youth. The senior pastor led a weekly small group with juniors and seniors and taught a class in the children's ministry. The associate minister taught a class for the high school students. The youth pastor preached while the senior pastor was gone. Both the associate minister and the youth pastor led worship while the worship pastor was gone. When the need arose, this group of specialists, because of the nature of their involvement with one another, became generalists to meet the needs of their ministries.

What Faithful Teammates Do

Faithful teammates are coworkers with a common interest in the unity and success of the team. Paul called these friends who were working with him by several names. He called Mark, Aristarchus, Demas, and Luke fellow workers (Philemon 24). He referred to Philemon as a partner (Philemon 17). Tychicus and Titus received double praise—Tychicus of being a faithful minister and fellow servant (Colossians 4:7), Titus of being a partner and fellow worker (2 Corinthians 8:23). Such people demonstrate the value of being faithfully aligned with fellow servants in ministry.

Help One Another in Ministry

First, faithful teammates help one another by contributing something to the benefit of the group. Paul instructed Timothy, "Get Mark and bring him with you, because he is helpful to me in my ministry" (2 Timothy 4:11). Mark offered Paul's ministry some assistance that was noticeably missing when Mark was away. The same could be said of Mordecai, who functioned in a similar role as Esther's helpful partner. He provided wisdom and counsel, gave Esther information about her enemy, offered prayerful support, and fasted with Esther. Without envy or selfish ambition, Mordecai understood his behind-the-scenes, yet influential, role that changed the fate of the Jewish people. Without his assistance Esther might not have saved her people. (See Esther 2:7, 10-11, 20; 3:7, 12-17.)

How many of us recall with dread those group assignments that we had to do throughout school? Invariably, someone would not do his share of the work. A teammate who has nothing to contribute to help the group meet its objectives not only is functionally useless, she is also destructive to the morale of those who end up shouldering more responsibility. This is true of school projects, and it is true for church ministry as well.

Implicit in the role of a teammate is a responsibility to be helpful to others on the team. In this light, youth ministry volunteers are never just van drivers, they are teammates contributing to the mission. A youth pastor in a church leadership meeting is not a coy chair-warmer, she is a contributor to the communal vision and work of ministry. At times you may not be in a position to offer anything but verbal support for someone else. For the sake of the team, that verbal support should not be withheld.

Paul did exactly this for his teammate Phoebe. He commended her to the Christians in Rome as a sister and a servant worthy of a saint's reception. Paul instructed the Romans to give Phoebe "any help she may need . . . for she has been a great help to many people, including me" (Romans 16:2). Paul ensured that the Roman church knew how special Phoebe was to him. She had served many people, and Paul was going to let them know about it.

Vouch for Each Other's Ministries

A second trait of faithful teammates is their willingness to serve as witnesses to each other's lives and ministries. Paul continually lavished praise on those he worked with. One of these men was Epaphras. Paul told the Colossians that Epaphras "is always wrestling in prayer for you" (Colossians 4:12). He added, "I vouch for [Epaphras] that he is working hard for you and for those at Laodicea and Hierapolis" (4:13). By praising the work of this teammate Paul elevated him before the people he served, which certainly helped Epaphras's ministry.

In the final chapter of Romans, we find Paul boasting about the work of many of his fellow workers: He names Mary (Romans 16:6), Tryphena and Tryphosa (16:12), and Persis (16:12) as women who work "very hard in the Lord." These accolades are not just kind words spoken to endear Paul to those about whom they were written. His praise testifies to the diligent perseverance of the workers who had labored together with him, even in times of adversity.

Endure Opposition Together

Third, faithful teammates strive together in the face of opposition. Paul told the Philippians to assist Euodia and Synthyche who had struggled beside him (Philippians 4:2-3). Priscilla and Aquila risked their lives for Paul (Romans 16:3). The Ephesians seized Gaius and Aristarchus because of their association with Paul (Acts 19:29), and Aristarchus was imprisoned with him (Colossians 4:10). For Paul to say that Euodia and Synthyche struggled beside him places them in the company of those who almost died because of their service.

Comfort Each Other

Faithful teammates do more than work beside their fellow servants. They also comfort one another. Speaking of his teammates to the Colossians, Paul said, "My fellow workers . . . have proved a comfort to me" (Colossians 4:11). Their presence and encouragement heartened Paul. They reminded him that he was not serving in a vacuum, that there were others laboring with him.

Youth ministry will bring days of loneliness when you do not really feel like part of a team. It may be after a long summer of trips away from your family or during a period of fatigue and introspection. Sometimes you may feel like you are the only one able or willing to invest energy into the mission of loving youth.

Remember that Elijah felt alone but was part of a cohort of 7,000 people who, like him, claimed God as the Lord, refusing to bow down to Baal. For some reason he could not see these faithful teammates, but that reminder from God propelled him back into exercising his responsibilities as a prophet (1 Kings 19:14-18).

Represent the Group on Behalf of Others

A fifth characteristic of faithful teammates is their ability to represent the team in the presence of others. Several servants on Paul's team functioned in this way for him. Epaphras served on Paul's behalf among the Colossians (Colossians 4:12-13); Paul sent Timothy to Corinth to demonstrate Paul's way of living (1 Corinthians 4:17). Titus also represented Paul in Corinth (2 Corinthians 8:23), as well as on Crete (Titus 1:5). While Titus was serving on that island, Paul told him to be careful in teaching, "so that those who oppose you may be ashamed because they have nothing bad to say about us" (Titus 2:8). Paul associated himself so closely with Titus's message and teaching that those who opposed Titus also set themselves against Paul.

Submit to One Another

Working together on a church staff is an excellent opportunity to live out the "one another" commandments that seem so good in theory, but are difficult in practice: serve one another, love one another, submit to one another. Supporting others to improve their service and contributing to the team's mission may conflict with our human tendency to seek individual praise. Teamwork demands some degree of personal sacrifice for the sake of the ultimate goal. John the Baptist understood this and knew that his ministry was not about him at all. This allowed him to point others, even his own disciples, to Jesus. When asked if it bothered him for hoards of people to be flocking to Jesus, he said, "He must become greater; I must become less" (John 3:30). His goal was to direct people to Christ. The kingdom of God was the focus, not John.

In the same way, our mission is bigger than we are. The church team, the staff, elders, leaders, and workers are a team working to build up the body of Christ. The parents, youth staff, interns, and volunteers are all working to bring youth into a growing relationship with God through Christ. When we fully buy in to this objective, our own position becomes insignificant. This is important to remember, especially if you feel like your service is not appreciated. Often in lists of ministries and ministers our names and positions are found near the bottom of the list, and this is not just because youth ministry starts with a "Y" and is last alphabetically. To enter youth ministry is often to take the lowest seat at the table. Others will be seated at places of more prominence in the eyes of church leadership and will therefore receive more recognition. It takes humility to work in youth ministry, knowing both how some people perceive the work and yet how influential the ministry really is. It is in the best interest of others, as well as the mission, to support and encourage others, to make them look good and to give them credit for their hard work and successes. Furthermore, when we take this humble position we might actually learn something along the way that helps us grow.

Actions of the Unfaithful

There are two specific threats to the relationships and unity of purpose that hold teams together. The first is the betrayal that results from carelessness of speech. David felt the sting of this duplicity when he wrote in the Psalms, "If an enemy were insulting me, I could endure it; if a foe were raising himself against me, I could hide from him. But it is you, a man like myself, my companion, my close friend, with whom I once enjoyed sweet fellowship as we walked with the throng at the house of God" (Psalm 55:12-14). A friend can become an enemy simply through careless words. Belittling, slandering, or gossiping about a coworker and expecting that person to be OK with it is like cracking an eggshell and expecting the egg to remain intact. It may hold together for a while but sooner or later things start to stink. Thoughtless murmurings have irreparably split many ministry teams.

A second type of betrayal happens when a member's actions oppose or hinder the efforts of the group. Like Judas who set himself against the purposes of his teacher for financial gain, some rogue teammates act out of selfish desires and do more harm than good to a team. David also wrote, "My companion attacks his friends; he violates his covenant" (Psalm 55:20) and "Even my close friend, whom I trusted, he who shared my bread, has lifted up his heel against me" (41:9). Jesus may have thought of that psalm as he watched Judas approaching to betray him. While not as sinister, Mark became untrustworthy to Paul because he had "deserted them in Pamphylia and had not continued with them in the work" (Acts 15:38). This lack of faithfulness resulted in Mark forfeiting his place on a future team with Paul.

What athletic teammates do in competition is a reflection of the patterns they have established while in practice. In the same way, effective church teams will possess an off-the-court rapport with one another that improves their service. This was what was missing between Paul and Mark.

I went to interview with a church once and had a great weekend. The teens were amazing, the parents encouraging, and the church leadership inspiring. I was certain this church would be a great match for my family until I met the senior minister. Over the course of a three-hour lunch he lectured me on what it meant to be a teammate and looked on me with a critical eye and a chip on his shoulder from past experiences with others. Sensing his cynicism, I asked what it was that he wanted from me. He said he just wanted to make sure I would be a team player. I explained to him that I felt like he was not giving me a chance to demonstrate my willingness to serve before he pushed me away. I turned down the job. Ironically, that senior minister was let go ten months later for his inability to work together with the rest of the staff. You are not a faithful teammate because you say you are. Faithful teammates have received that designation from those whom they work with.

Jesus, A Faithful Teammate With God

Jesus demonstrated what it means to be a faithful teammate while serving as a coworker with God the Father. First, Jesus and God, as two persons of the Trinity, helped each other in ministry while advancing the Kingdom. Jesus did God's will on earth and God helped Jesus by providing for his needs, answering his prayers, and sending angels to attend him. Second, God the Father testified to the validity of Jesus' ministry when he spoke from heaven saying, "This is my Son, whom I love; with him I am well pleased" (Matthew 3:17; 17:5). Jesus vouched for God's intentions as he told people about God's love. Third, the Father and the Son endured opposition together as they moved toward the mutual goal of God's glorification. Specifically, during his temptation in the wilderness and while praying in the garden of Gethsemane, Jesus labored to remain focused on the purpose for his life. Fourth, Jesus was comforted by the presence of God's Holy Spirit in his life. Jesus also represented God among the people. He prayed, "You are in me and I am in you" (John 17:21), indicating that he and his heavenly Father functioned as one entity. Jesus fulfilled this existence by living as Immanuel, "God with us." Finally, Jesus submitted to God as he prayed, "Not my will, but yours be done" (Luke 22:42).

Jesus' teamwork with God the Father set an example for other teams. Jesus said that such teamwork, cooperation, and unity would testify to God's love for the world (John 17:23). And Jesus prayed that his followers would be one just as Jesus was one with God (17:22). As one entity, Jesus and God share all things in common. Thus Jesus could pray, "All I have is yours, and all you have is mine" (17:10). The Book of Acts shows us how the early church imitated this mutuality as no one claimed that any of his possessions were his own, but gave freely to anyone who was in need (Acts 4:32-37).

Unity in Diversity

On his third missionary journey, Paul left Ephesus (in the province of Asia) to visit Macedonia. Luke records the names of Paul's team on this trip (Acts 20:4). It is a diverse list that included men from various cities: Sopater from Berea, Aristarchus and

Secundus from Thessalonica, Gaius from Derbe, Timothy from Lystra (16:1), Trophimus from Ephesus (21:29), and Tychicus from the province of Asia. As a microcosm of the body of Christ, this team included people of assorted backgrounds.

Youth pastors may find themselves on teams as diverse as Paul's crew. We find ourselves in groups that include people who may be older, younger, more educated, less experienced, new to faith, bold in prayer, and peaceful in conflict. Such differences are hardly deficiencies. They can actually work to strengthen the group. Each person has a unique gift that contributes to the mosaic of ministry. For this reason, each teammate should be familiar with everyone else's job, and each should serve as an understudy for someone else. In the event of an emergency, one teammate can help or cover for another. Working in concert with others toward the same goal not only moves the team closer to a desired end, but it also testifies to the unity of God. When God created humans, God said, "Let us make man in our image" (Genesis 1:26). It was a team effort with contributions from not only God the Father, but Jesus and the Holy Spirit as well. We imitate that model as we work with one another in the church.

Lessons From the Community Wall

As we have seen, sometimes you are on a team precisely because your special giftedness serves the group's purpose. You may be good at teaching junior high students. Maybe you connect well with fringe kids. You might know all the cool bands that teens listen to. You could be really great at leading worship. Whatever your area of specialization, your specialty gives you an identity and a sense of security as part of the team.

Other times loyalty to a team does not take giftedness into account. Instead, the objective of the team takes priority over any one participant's area of expertise. As valuable as each unique member of the community is, there may be times when the community needs the help of every member, regardless of her gifts; a time when the objectives of the group outweigh the preferences or unique skills of the individual.

This was the situation for the citizens of Jerusalem when Nehemiah gained permission to rebuild the city of his ancestors.

Almost every member of the community helped rebuild the wall of Jerusalem. Some built gates, while others rebuilt entire sections, and still others simply worked opposite their own homes to reinforce the city's defenses. The list of those who served is impressive: goldsmiths (Nehemiah 3:8, 31), merchants (3:32), perfume-makers (3:8), rulers of districts (3:9, 12, 14, 15, 19), daughters (3:12), Levites (3:17), priests (3:28), the high priest (3:1), the countrymen (3:18), men from other cities (3:2, 7, 13, 27), priests from the surrounding region (3:22), the temple servants (3:26), and the guard of the East Gate (3:29).

Such a list might lead us to ask how our youth ministry teams reflect this diversity. We might also ask whether our mission is compelling enough to excite the enthusiasm and urgency of a people rebuilding their only line of defense for their families. When volunteers consider service in the youth ministry what purpose are they supporting, and do they even know?

Nehemiah rallied an eclectic list of wall-workers, but one group did not join the effort. The men of Tekoa repaired one section of the wall, "but their nobles would not put their shoulders to the work" (Nehemiah 3:5). These aristocrats refused to submit to the leadership of their supervisors, who were likely of lower social status. They would not bend and lower themselves from their lofty positions to join God's people in a historic event that would be remembered for thousands of years. The result was temporal self-righteousness but millennial disgrace. The nobles of Tekoa could have been listed with the humble servants who set out to rebuild the wall but are remembered instead as the project's sole opponents in Judah. When the story is told of the Kingdom work in your context, whose names will be listed as faithful teammates who put their shoulders to the work?

Reflection

1. How and why is teamwork vital to the success of church ministry?

2. Who are your teammates?

3. What are your team's goals? What are you trying to accomplish?

4. What actions or conversations have hindered the unity of the team you are on? How has sin affected your team?

5. What tasks currently handled by teammates would you have difficulty covering if there were an emergency? What can you do to learn these responsibilities?

6. What actions could you take (or what changes in attitude could you make) in the interest of a more unified ministry team?

CHAPTER TWELVE
Discover Your Ministry Style

Being a youth pastor is not easy. As we established in the first chapter, youth ministry requires skillfully juggling diverse roles in dissimilar contexts with people of multiple generations while enlisting volunteers to join the effort. Effective leadership in these conditions means altering your approach for each unique situation you encounter. Jesus was masterful at this. He was gentle at the appropriate time but assertive when the situation demanded it. He could encourage a small child and rebuke religious leaders. In the same way, youth ministry involves knowing what roles are required for a given situation and which ones should take priority at any given time. Making these types of judgments begins by considering our own patterns of service in youth ministry.

Personal Tendencies: What is your ministry style?

The ten roles presented in this book function as a mirror for self-discovery in youth ministry by helping us reflect on who we are as youth pastors. Youth ministry requires us to move among these roles for the spiritual benefit of teens and their families. As Ecclesiastes reminds us, "There is a time for everything, and a season for every activity under heaven" (3:1). Youth pastors should be able to read the seasons and tell the time in order to respond appropriately in every situation. As we do this we will likely discover that we are drawn to some roles more than others. To discover these tendencies consider the following questions:

- Which of the roles do I most enjoy?
- What aspects of ministry energize me?

- Which of these do I prefer spending my time on?
- How have I spent my time during the last week, month, and year?
- What have people said about my abilities that point to areas of giftedness?

Look at the Youth Ministry Style Profile on page 147. For each role circle the number that best describes your tendencies as a youth pastor in this role, with 1 representing Slight Tendencies and 5 representing Strong Tendencies. Note that the ranking for roles on the left moves from 5 (Strong Tendencies) to 1 (Slight Tendencies), while the ranking for roles on the right moves from 1 (Slight Tendencies) to 5 (Strong Tendencies). A more descriptive look at each role is provided in the Appendix if you are not sure where you land on the continuum.

This typology requires some clarification. First, this exercise is not intended to be a definitive assessment of giftedness, but rather a reflection of your preferred style of doing youth ministry. Our future service as youth pastors does not depend on how we fare with this inventory. God can use us in any way that God wills, even in areas where we feel unqualified (think Moses' objections in Exodus 4:10). And remember Paul, the formerly zealous Pharisee who condoned the murder of Christians. He became something entirely different when he encountered Jesus. We may experience a similar transfiguration as we grow in our relationship with God.

Second, though I have presented these roles as pairs—as opposite ends of a continuum—this dichotomy is artificial. Serving as a spiritual friend to teens and an equipping recruiter of adults should not be mutually exclusive. Ministers often play many roles simultaneously. This happened to Moses as he negotiated a conversation between God and Israel. After receiving the Law from God, Moses acted as a prophet and "set before them all the words the Lord had commanded him to speak" (Exodus 19:7). In the very next verse, Moses takes on a priestly role, representing the people before God when "Moses brought their answer back to the Lord" (19:8). Likewise, we may have to manage overlapping roles in youth ministry.

By evaluating our preferences for certain roles we gain valuable information that can improve our ministry service. First, we may

Youth Ministry Style Profile

EVANGELISTIC MISSIONARY				
5	4	3	2	1
Strong Tendencies		Moderate Tendencies		Slight Tendencies

				DISCIPLING TEACHER
1	2	3	4	5
Slight Tendencies		Moderate Tendencies		Strong Tendencies

PASTORAL SHEPHERD				
5	4	3	2	1
Strong Tendencies		Moderate Tendencies		Slight Tendencies

				ORGANIZED ADMINISTRATOR
1	2	3	4	5
Slight Tendencies		Moderate Tendencies		Strong Tendencies

BOLD PROPHET				
5	4	3	2	1
Strong Tendencies		Moderate Tendencies		Slight Tendencies

				COMPASSIONATE PRIEST
1	2	3	4	5
Slight Tendencies		Moderate Tendencies		Strong Tendencies

SPIRITUAL FRIEND				
5	4	3	2	1
Strong Tendencies		Moderate Tendencies		Slight Tendencies

				EQUIPPING RECRUITER
1	2	3	4	5
Slight Tendencies		Moderate Tendencies		Strong Tendencies

VISIONARY LEADER				
5	4	3	2	1
Strong Tendencies		Moderate Tendencies		Slight Tendencies

				FAITHFUL TEAMMATE
1	2	3	4	5
Slight Tendencies		Moderate Tendencies		Strong Tendencies

discover that we are more inclined to certain roles. These inclinations should be celebrated as gifts from God. God blesses servants with interests, passions, and skills to equip them for their roles; but areas of perceived strength can become weaknesses if they are practiced to the exclusion of other, complementary roles. For example, those who are skillful as bold prophets, proclaiming the truth of God's message to teens, may lose an audience if they cannot learn compassion for those with whom they speak. As a result, a strength is rendered ineffective. For this reason, we might also consider how to grow into the roles we are less inclined to take on and to incorporate these roles more effectively into our ministries.

Remember the words that Paul used to describe his willingness to play a variety of roles for the sake of others: "Though I am free and belong to no man, I make myself a slave to everyone. . . . I do all this for the sake of the gospel" (1 Corinthians 9:19, 23). Paul probably did not enjoy becoming like one under the law again (as he had been during his days as a Pharisee), but he did it because of his ultimate objective: to reach as many as possible. We may not enjoy some roles as much as others, but we cannot for that reason neglect them. The flexibility required to transition among several roles, as Paul did, takes effort, persistence, and work. It may require setting goals for personal development, learning from a mentor who is skilled in roles that we are less inclined to take on, and praying for God to help us acquire certain proficiencies. As we navigate our own tendencies and personal ministry style, we should keep in mind that other variables influence decisions about what roles we must play to be effective youth ministers. These include the ministry context, a church's expectations, and gifts of volunteers.

Ministry Context: What does your ministry need?

It is unhealthy to transport a youth ministry program from one church into other contexts because each group of people and each environment is unique. "One size fits all" does not apply (Chow, 19). Differences in the size of the youth ministry, the collective character of the teens and families, and the specific needs of those being served determine which roles are most crucial. But the youth pastor should never be left to discern these things on her own. The community will also determine what the ministry needs.

Church Expectations: What do others believe is important?

Several groups of people—including elders, staff members, parents, and teens—have expectations about the youth pastor's role that we must seriously consider. This is not to say that we should always give others what they want. The parents may say that they want a spiritual friend of teens more than an equipping recruiter of adults, while their teens are not forming significant relationships with adults in the church and the youth pastor is spiritually exhausted from the burden of doing too much by himself. In this case what the parents want will only be accomplished when they realize what they need: more adult involvement in the ministry.

Because unmet expectations often produce conflict, it is vital to understand employers' expectations before accepting a ministry position. For that reason, as churches consider potential pastors, they might reflect on their expectations for this role and compare their expectations to the tendencies of the applicants. This would open dialogue that could prevent a mismatch between pastor and church and help lead the right person to a ministry.

I shared these ten roles with a group of adult volunteers in my church and asked them to circle the one role in each dyad that most described what they wanted from their youth pastor. As we tallied the group's responses, we found that my tendencies only matched their expectations in 3 of the 5 areas. That initiated a discussion about the role of the youth pastor and the ultimate goals of the ministry. This exercise clearly illustrated that one person, namely the youth pastor, was not capable of serving in all of these roles at all times for all teens.

Volunteer Tendencies: What are your volunteers' styles?

The challenge for youth pastors is not only to understand their inclinations and take on various roles when appropriate but also to recruit others who complement their tendencies. Numerous adults are needed to play all the roles necessary for a healthy youth ministry. When we define our tendencies and preferences and those of the other adults who are involved in our ministry, we are better suited to recruit additional adults who bring gifts that supplement those already present. For this to work, adult volunteers must discern and name their interests and the roles they are drawn to in ministry. Toward this end you might invite your parents and adult volunteers to complete the Youth Ministry Style Profile (above). Once you have information about their inclinations, you can recruit those adults who complement others on the team or whose tendencies match specific ministry needs.

By assessing how we spend our time and which areas of ministry come naturally, youth pastors are able to spend more time on our strengths while giving special attention to those areas of ministry that do not come to us naturally. We will be able to see how our ministry style preferences correspond to the needs of the ministry and the expectations of others invested in the ministry. We will gain insight that will help us recruit volunteers. Finally, we can gauge success by comparing the objectives of each role against progress we have made in that area. Instead of focusing on the number of teens in our program or whether we have enough activities to keep the middle school students out of trouble, we can focus on the foundation of our service as youth pastors: our relationship with God and our relationships with youth and their families.

Reflection

1. How do the results from the Youth Ministry Style Profile inform how you do ministry?

2. What can you do to ensure that your areas of less inclination are represented in your ministry?

3. How do the styles of other leaders in the youth ministry compare to your ministry style?

4. What are the strengths of your ministry style? What have you been able to accomplish because of how God has uniquely gifted you?

Note

Chow, David. 2005. *The perfect program and other fairy tales: Confessions of a well-intentioned youth worker.* Colorado Springs, CO: Th1nk.

Character and Competence in Ministry

Several years ago I attended a youth pastor's retreat with ten area ministers where a professor from a Christian university spoke about ministry. This professor talked about spiritual formation and the joy of living with an awareness of God's presence as we serve in ministry. At one point a youth pastor asked the professor about personal formation and what it would look like for youth pastors to do the things he was discussing. Specifically, what would it look like to imitate the life of Jesus in ministry? After a brief pause this professor suggested beginning with at least 30 to 45 minutes of personal Bible study and prayer every day, then outlining one's daily tasks in order of importance based on the mission and vision of one's ministry. Surprisingly, one youth pastor interjected, "Well, I don't even get to the office until 11 a.m. so I could just do that stuff and then go to lunch!" The incompetent minority had spoken. And I do believe that it is a minority of youth pastors who would do something as foolish as to consistently arrive late to work. That sort of immaturity is hardly appropriate for our vocation.

Youth ministry is the Spirit-led discipleship process by which Christian adults lead teens into relationship with God and Christlike maturity in the church. That type of mission requires hearts that are attentive to God and hands that are skillful at the work they do. Whatever our tendencies might be, youth ministry demands character and competence. These are central to youth ministry training (Rahn 1996, 81) and nonnegotiable for day-to-day ministry.

Character

When it comes to ministry, "proven character must precede position" (Hegg 1998, 37). Those in the church will closely observe the example we set by our lives, our integrity, and our daily living. This gives us an opportunity to set an example of righteous living, modeling what we would like others to become. This also requires integrity, "the consistency between what we say and what we do. Following through on promises made, saying the same thing to different people about an incident, and . . . setting an example are all ways of showing this consistency" (Hobgood 1998, 33). Every day we make choices that both reflect and shape our character. This is not to suggest youth ministers should be stoic and polished, espousing unrealistic perfection. That would be of no benefit. Rather, while pursuing the character of Jesus, we can admit failures, and refocus on our goal after we have been distracted. A life of integrity is rarely achieved without intentionality. Such a life is the result of continual attention to the desired goal of formation in the image of Christ. Our character is forged in the fire of self-discipline and consistency.

Daniel had character. He consistently was faithful to God, and it was this dependability that his coworkers used against him. The other officials came up with a plan to trap Daniel by making a law that anyone who prayed to any god or man except King Darius would be thrown into the lions' den. So what did Daniel do? "When Daniel learned that the decree had been published, he went home to his upstairs room where the windows opened toward Jerusalem. Three times a day he got down on his knees and prayed, giving thanks to his God, just as he had done before" (Daniel 6:10). It has been said that character is who you are when no one is looking, and we can learn a lot about ourselves by asking, "What do I do when I am alone?" But character is more than that. Character is who you are when *everyone* is looking. Daniel was consistent in worshiping God, even when he knew that the royal administrators would be watching and even when he knew that the consequence of his action would likely be death.

Our lives are a continuation of the story written by great people such as Daniel, but sometimes our chapters are not as impressive. Some days we are like Nehemiah, who refused to sin because it would have discredited him in his leadership (Nehemiah 6:13). But if we are honest other days we are more like Achan, who was irresponsible with objects devoted to God (Joshua 7:1). Like Paul we find ourselves engaged in what we do not want to do, while wishing we were doing something else (Romans 7:15). We may look back with regret at wasted time. Or perhaps there were times when we should have remained silent because our words were hurtful. Or times when we remained silent even though justice demanded that we speak up. But instead of letting imperfections paralyze us, we can choose to continue pursuing Christlikeness with God's help.

Competence

If character is a prerequisite for a position in ministry, competence is the qualification for continuing in ministry. Daniel not only maintained his integrity while serving, he also demonstrated competence and his exceptional qualities set him apart from his peers. "He was trustworthy and neither corrupt [in character] nor negligent [in competence]" (Daniel 6:4). You could count on Daniel because he was not only good as a person, but he was also good at his job. He paid attention in Administration 101. He probably watched those who went before him, learned from them, and continued learning once he was in a position of influence. In short, he was intentional about serving well. He understood that quality work is never an accident, and it is never the result of laziness. In the same way, competency in youth ministry is rarely an accident. It is usually the result of focused attention to purpose, execution, and details along the way. A competent youth pastor will be responsible with the time, teens, and talents entrusted to her care.

Spiritual Disciplines

One of the ways we develop consistent character is to consistently engage in activities that develop character. In the same way, to develop competence in ministry we should engage in activities that benefit ministry service. Through consistent practice we can train ourselves with habits that produce character and competence in ministry. The spiritual disciplines function as tools to assist this process. By engaging in these activities, we place ourselves in God's presence and submit to the work of God's transforming Spirit.

The practices of a Spirit-filled life not only tend our souls to produce hearts that are attentive to God, but they also equip us with resources for ministry. "There is a link between character and competence that makes character and competence complementary. A person who desires to please God in ministry will desire to acquire those skills that make one an effective instrument for God. On the other hand, the skills required of ministry . . . reinforce our love of God and form us into more godly people" (Willimon 2000, 41). Both our character and our competence are formed through these practices.

A list provided below illustrates some of the ways in which spiritual disciplines inform and contribute to the roles required for youth ministry service. Some disciplines are uniquely evident in specific roles, such as fasting, which bold prophets Moses, Elijah, and Jesus all did for extended periods. But fasting is not just a discipline for bold prophets. Fasting also could serve priests who want to sympathize with the pain of the people. Some disciplines naturally correspond to multiple roles, and two disciplines inform all aspects of ministry service: prayer and teaching.

ROLES	SPIRITUAL DISCIPLINES
Evangelistic Missionary	Testimony, Journaling, Teaching, Hospitality
Discipling Teacher	Teaching, Study, Prayer, Journaling
Pastoral Shepherd	Compassion, Fellowship, Resting, Teaching
Organized Administrator	Solitude, Silence, Tithing, Ordering
Bold Prophet	Teaching, Accountability, Fasting, Simplicity
Compassionate Priest	Prayer, Worship, Sacrifice, Blessing, Confession
Spiritual Friend	Listening, Guidance, Celebration, Hospitality
Equipping Recruiter	Service, Training, Fellowship, Encouragement
Visionary Leader	Meditation, Prayer, Creating, Encouragement
Faithful Teammate	Submission, Service, Fellowship, Accountability

By placing ourselves in the presence of God through these practices, we emerge with renewed understanding of who we are as God's servants. We see more clearly who we are functionally in ministry and who we are deep within our souls. These insights into our character produce the humility to serve. Our competence produces the confidence to lead. The result is servant leadership.

As we serve, may we be

> confident without being arrogant,
> bold without being insensitive,
> sensitive without being fragile,
> faithful without being pious,
> submissive without being weak,
> humble without being self-deprecating, and
> holy without being self-righteous.

May we aspire to take on the qualities of the faithful servants who went before us, of whom it was said, "the world was not worthy of them" (Hebrews 11:38). And may our service follow in the lineage of David, whose character and competence guided his relationship with Israel: "David shepherded them with integrity of heart; with skillful hands he led them" (Psalm 78:72).

Reflection

1. Who serves as a model of character and competence in ministry for you?

2. What steps could you take to develop a more consistent character? What about competence?

3. How have the spiritual disciplines helped you mature in your relationship with Christ? How have they influenced your work as a youth pastor?

Notes

Hegg, David W. 1998. Proven character: Prelude to position. *Reformation and Revival Journal.* 7 (1): 35-55.

Hobgood, William Chris. 1998. *The once and future pastor: The changing role of religious leaders.* Herndon, VA: The Alban Institute.

Rahn, Dave. 1996. What kind of education do youth ministers need? *Christian Education Journal.* 16 (3): 81-89.

Willimon, William H. 2000. *Calling and character: Virtues of the ordained life.* Nashville, TN: Abingdon.

APPENDIX

YOUTH MINISTRY ROLE INVENTORY

Evangelistic Missionary

__ The thought of studying the Bible with a new Christian makes me more excited than nervous.

__ I frequently tell people about how I see God working.

__ My heart is filled with compassion for those who do not know Jesus.

__ I enjoy learning about youth culture.

Discipling Teacher

__ I enjoy preparing, studying for, and presenting lessons.

__ I get excited about sharing insights I have discovered from Scripture.

__ Helping Christians mature in their faith is a priority in my life.

__ I spend most of my time with other Christians.

Pastoral Shepherd

__ Some of my best work with people happens outside the office.

__ I feel a burden of responsibility for teens who are struggling in their relationship with God.

__ When people are not at church I am likely to let them know that they were missed.

__ I enjoy helping the teens I know become a unified group that functions as a community.

Organized Administrator

__ Some of my best work happens in a clean office because clutter slows me down.
__ I find myself wanting to discuss dates for events far in advance.
__ I like planning events and activities to ensure that they are done well.
__ I am more likely to have a curriculum series planned in advance than to decide week-to-week what I will teach.

Bold Prophet

__ I am passionate about defending those who are oppressed.
__ I feel convicted to expose sin and wickedness.
__ I enjoy prayer as a chance to be still in the presence of God.
__ I enjoy helping people see God's promises for their future.

Compassionate Priest

__ I enjoy prayer as a chance to intercede on behalf of others.
__ I feel deep compassion for people who are hurting and need healing and forgiveness.
__ I frequently bless or affirm people for the gifts I see in them.
__ I enjoy leading people in worship with songs, Scriptures, and experiences that help people encounter God.

Spiritual Friend

__ I like knowing that teens are encouraged because of me.
__ I frequently spend time with teens at their schools, in their homes, and at sporting events.
__ I would rather spend time with teens than with adult volunteers.
__ Teens come to me for advice and I frequently counsel them.

Equipping Recruiter

__ I enjoy searching for the right person to fit volunteer opportunities in ministry.

__ I consider spending time with parents as a primary focus of youth ministry.
__ I would rather spend time with adult volunteers than with teens.
__ I enjoy leading training and equipping sessions for volunteers in which I equip them with ministry resources.

Visionary Leader

__ I rarely serve in roles outside of youth ministry.
__ The responsibility I feel for the youth ministry program occupies most of my time at work.
__ I have great dreams and creative ideas that I would like to implement in the youth ministry.
__ I consider myself a specialist who focuses primarily on youth ministry.

Faithful Teammate

__ I enjoy the chance to do tasks outside my primary ministry area.
__ My loyalty to a church staff and leadership supersedes my loyalty to a particular ministry.
__ I frequently cover ministry tasks for fellow staff members on short notice.
__ I consider myself a ministry generalist who serves in many areas.

Acknowledgments

This work would not have been possible without the generous support of my wife Karen. She has been my ministry companion and conversation partner as we served God together. It has been my great joy to watch Matalee, Emery, and Haven become the recipients of your inspiring gift as a discipling teacher of their young hearts.

I cannot express sufficient thanks to Jenny Youngman for her vision and faith in this project and to Josh Tinley for his leadership and editorial contributions to this work. I am also grateful to Casey McCollum and Karen Houdashell for their willingness to read and respond to many of these thoughts as they were developing.

There are those who, perhaps unknowingly, have made significant contributions to this book through our conversations about ministry. For your friendship and partnership in the gospel I am grateful: Chris Hatchett, Robert Oglesby, David Wray, Glenn Pemberton, Charles Siburt, and Slade Sullivan. Thank you also to Dan Stevens and John Siburt, my faithful teammates in church ministry. Our journey together has been a blessing.

Finally, thank you to the One whose generosity has given me life and breath and everything else. May these words contribute to your praise.

Houston Heflin